THE PRIORITY OF MIND

THE PRIORITY OF MIND

Keith Ward

CASCADE *Books* · Eugene, Oregon

THE PRIORITY OF MIND

Cascade Books
An Imprint of Wipf and Stock Publishers
199 W. 8th Ave., Suite 3
Eugene, OR 97401
www.wipfandstock.com

PAPERBACK ISBN: 978-1-6667-3528-4
HARDCOVER ISBN: 978-1-6667-9220-1
EBOOK ISBN: 978-1-6667-9221-8

Cataloging-in-Publication data:

Names: Ward, Keith, 1938– [author]

Title: The priority of mind / by Keith Ward.

Description: Eugene, OR : Cascade Books, 2021 | Includes bibliographical references.

Identifiers: ISBN 978-1-6667-3528-4 (paperback) | ISBN 978-1-6667-9220-1 (hardcover) | ISBN 978-1-6667-9221-8 (ebook)

Subjects: LCSH: Idealism | Mind and body | Philosophy of mind | Philosophy and religion | Life—Religious aspects | Meaning (Philosophy)—Religious aspects | Immaterialism (Philosophy)

Classification: LCC BR100 W37 2021 (print) | LCC BR100 (ebook)

VERSION NUMBER 110121

CONTENTS

INTRODUCTION

A few years ago, Richard Dawkins wrote a best-selling book, *The Selfish Gene* (Boulder, CO: Paladin, 1976). It was a really well-written book, with lots of fascinating facts in it, by a well-respected zoologist at Oxford University. And yet it was almost completely wrong.

I need to amend that statement at once. The biological facts in it were not wrong. So it was not really *completely* wrong. In fact, it was a brilliant and illuminating account of evolutionary biology. But what was wrong was very important. It was the impression it gave, and that it *meant* to give, that you, and all human beings, are animals that have evolved by chance. There is no intelligent direction or purpose that got you here. You are composed of particles of matter that operate in accordance with blind laws of nature, and just happen to have produced you. You are some sort of accident of nature. In a later book, Professor Dawkins wrote, "There is, at bottom, no design, no purpose, no evil and no good, nothing but blind pitiless indifference" (*River Out of Eden* [New York: Basic, 1993], 133).

You may think you are an intelligent, free, responsible agent. But, in fact, you are simply a machine controlled by your basic particles, your genes, and the smaller physical unthinking bits and pieces of which genes are made. Dawkins writes, "we are survival machines—robot vehicles blindly programmed to preserve the selfish molecules known as genes" (Dawkins, *The Selfish Gene*, x). There is no reason why you exist; there is no point in your existence, and you are certainly not the high-point of creation, somehow more important than all the other animals.

I think that this is a significantly wrong picture of what you really are. I want to persuade you that it is a lopsided picture. It misses out all that is most important about being human. Its picture of human life and of the universe in which humans exist is in fact almost completely upside down.

This might seem to be a very rash claim of mine. Does it not fly in the face of everything modern science tells us? I do not think so. In fact, I am going to argue that modern science has a very different story to tell. And I am going to try to tell it.

I suppose I should start by saying something about who I am. This may seem rather egotistical, but it is important these days to know if an author is the genuine article. I am certainly not infallible, but I am, I suppose one could say, well qualified in both philosophy and theology. After a short spell in the Royal Air Force, I became a university lecturer in philosophy at Glasgow University, then at St. Andrews University, and then at King's College, University of London. After that, I was dean of Trinity Hall, Cambridge and director of studies in philosophy and theology at Cambridge University, where I lectured in the philosophy faculty. Then I held the following chairs, one after the other: Professor of Moral Theology, then Professor of the History and Philosophy of Religion, at London University, Regius Professor of Divinity at Oxford University, Research Professor in Philosophy at Heythrop College, and Professor of Philosophy at Roehampton University. I eventually retired at eighty-two. I am a Fellow of the British Academy and an Emeritus Student (the Christ Church term for a Life Fellow) of Christ Church College, Oxford.

I am only reciting that rather boring list to show that at least I am professionally qualified in the subject I am writing about. I need to do this because I have tried not to write this book in an academic style. It has no footnotes, references, equations, or too many technical terms (though I could not resist adding a short appendix with some references for those who are interested). It is meant to be a serious work in philosophy, but it is written in a way that is not too serious. That is because I think it is a really important topic, so I wanted to make it readable to intelligent people who may not be professionally qualified.

This book is an attempt to persuade you of the truth of a philosophical view that I call "personal idealism." Idealism, in philosophy, is the belief that mind is more real than matter. Without mind, matter would not exist. The fundamental nature of reality is mind. There could not be a physical universe without mind as its basis. Extreme Idealists say that matter does not exist at all. Personal idealists accept that matter exists, but that it wholly depends upon mental reality. There is one basic supreme mind, and the whole physical universe is the expression and manifestation of that mind. As a mind, it has the personal characteristics of knowing, feeling, and willing. So, the universe is not really blind, pitiless, and indifferent. On the contrary, it is conscious, compassionate, and concerned for human well-being.

This idealist view is, I think, rather unfashionable nowadays, even though some form of it has been held by most classical philosophers from Plato onwards. I intend to join them in defending it.

I have divided this book into four parts. The first is a look at human minds and what they are really like. The second asks what the universe must be like if it has generated such minds. It assumes an evolutionary view and suggests that the universe must be mind-like. The third draws conclusions about how humans should act if personal idealism is true and agrees (in a slightly new way) with the time-honoured tradition that human well-being consists in seriously pursuing truth, beauty, and goodness. And the fourth spells out the implication that, if the basis of reality is mind, there is probably a life beyond physical death in which human minds can find some sort of conscious and creative unity with that cosmic mind.

Part One

MIND

1. THE SOURCES OF MIND

WHERE SHOULD I BEGIN? Let me begin by thinking about Professor Dawkins setting out to write a book called *The Selfish Gene*. He wrote the book after a lifetime of study and thinking. He learned to observe animal behavior and to read all about what many biologists before him had discovered about human bodies, cells, and genes. He had to learn how to observe things carefully, and how to read and understand the thoughts of many other people.

This is pretty obvious. It just means that human knowledge, *all* human knowledge, must begin with careful observation and logical thinking. Without observation (using our sense of sight, sound, touch, and so on) and without thinking (actively trying to understand how things work) there would be no knowledge about the universe at all.

We can put this in two simple sentences:

- "All knowledge begins with experience." And,

- "Experience can only be understood by concentrated mental effort."

As I say, pretty obvious. But what it says is very important. It says that experiences (sights, sounds, touches, smells, and sensations) must exist if we are to have any knowledge. And it says that processes of trying to think and understand (thought-processes) must exist as well.

We cannot accept any theory about human beings, or about anything else either, that does not accept that *experiences and thoughts exist*, and that they are the very *basis* of all our theories; they cannot under any circumstances be denied or ignored. Any theory that denies or ignores experiences and thoughts *must* be wrong.

Now, where do experiences and thoughts exist, and what are they made of? This might sound a very odd question, but the fact that it sounds odd is because we have probably been conned into thinking that experiences and thoughts are somehow in the brain. They are, we might have been persuaded, spin-offs from physical events (the firing of neurons) in the brain. They play no part in deciding what goes on. They are purely subjective happenings that scientists can safely ignore.

This is, I believe, is the biggest mistake that people like Professor Dawkins make. Because if experiences and thoughts actually exist, they are certainly not in the physical brain.

The human brain, as a physical thing, is about 1.5 kilograms of pinkish jelly-like tissue. You can take it out of the skull and cut it up, and you will not find any experiences or thoughts. You will find a hundred billion neurons, tiny brain-cells, which, when the brain is alive, send hundreds of electrical impulses to thousands of other neurons every second. You can attach electrodes to a living brain or scan it with complicated machines, to see how blood flows through it or what electro-chemical activity is going on in it. But you still will not find any experiences or thoughts.

To put it simply, the brain is a physical system—the most complicated one in the known universe—which is made up of fundamental particles that have properties like mass, electrical charge, location, and momentum. These are all physical properties that we can observe and measure. They exist in space, and can be detected by any competent person who knows how to spot them.

Now think of Professor Dawkins' brain hard at work as he writes his latest book. It will undoubtedly be a hive of activity, as neurons in the brain fire, blood flows through specific parts of the brain, and all sorts of electrical and chemical connections take place in an amazingly complex way throughout the brain. Just as we can in principle list all the physical processes that take place when a computer is calculating some difficult sum, so we could in principle list all the physical processes that take place in Professor Dawkins' brain when he is writing a book.

But there is a huge difference. With the computer, there are definite and describable rules that ensure that, given a certain input (say, hitting some keys on a keypad), a definite output will follow (say, specific letters appearing on a screen). But nobody will say the computer is thinking and deciding what to say next. The computer has no idea of what it is doing. It is just a machine. It does not know what the printed letters mean, and it never stops to wonder what letters it should print next. Everything is completely predetermined by the rules (though sometimes programmers could put in some random moves).

Professor Dawkins, however, unlike a computer, *does* know what he is doing. He no doubt often wonders just what to say next, and no doubt sometimes tries out a number of possibilities from which he consciously selects the one he prefers.

That is what thinking is. It is having an idea of what one wants to say, seeking out the best way of saying it, and composing a text which "feels right" and gives a feeling of satisfaction.

You are thinking right now. Just pause, sit quietly, and try to observe what is going on in your mind. Thoughts pass by, almost with a life of their own. But you can concentrate, change their direction, or just let them pass by. If you are thinking about what you have just read, you can try to decide whether you agree with it or not. You have a purpose—you want to know what you believe. You can try to come to a decision, to find the truth and avoid error. You have a sense of action and effort. And you have some sort of feeling, perhaps of puzzlement or annoyance or relief. Nobody else knows what is going on. This is your purpose, your active effort, and your feeling.

It is a purely mental action and purpose. It certainly exists, though it is not observable by anyone else.

2. THE BRAIN AND THE MIND

To change the example, think of Einstein inventing the theory of relativity. He is faced with the problem of explaining how physical objects seemingly act on one another at a distance (they attract each other by the force of gravity). He tries out several different explanations. But at some point, he hits on the idea that gravity is not really a force between two separate objects. It is a bending of space-time by objects with mass. This is an amazingly new idea that nobody had ever thought of before.

Now ask yourself the question: could somebody who knew everything about what was happening in Einstein's physical brain somehow observe his theory of bendy spacetime? That is, could they observe his thoughts?

The answer is obviously *no*. They could observe that his brain was active, that certain parts of it were especially active. They could possibly even observe that he was thinking about physics by seeing which regions of the brain were working. But they could not observe the theory of relativity. It is just not the sort of thing that could be observed.

Things like the theory of relativity or the theory of the selfish gene are not actually in the physical brain. They are not physical things. Yet they exist. The inescapable conclusion is that there are things that exist that are not in space, and that cannot be observed by any physical means.

It might seem at first to make sense to say that the selfish gene theory exists in Dawkins' brain. But that is only because we (some of us) have been deluded into thinking that everything that exists must exist in space and be observable in principle by every competent observer.

What I am driving at is that *thoughts do not exist in space.* They exist, as we normally say, in the *mind*. The mind is not the physical brain, though there is no doubt that, in the case of human beings anyway, the physical brain has to be active and working properly if there is to be anything going on in the mind.

Perhaps it is true that the mind is a spin-off from the physical brain. Indeed, in a sense, I agree that it is true. But even if it is true, the mind is still *real*. If you make a list of the sorts of things that exist, you will have to add minds to that list, in addition to physical things in space and time. That will turn out to be the first clue to seeing why a Dawkins view of human life is inadequate. He does not pay much attention to the mind, even though without it he could not know or understand or write anything. That failure to pay attention to minds will turn out to be very important when we try to understand what a human is.

If there are minds as well as brains, what sorts of things are in the mind? I have pointed out that thoughts are not in the physical brain. Neither are sounds, smells, tastes, touches, bodily sensations (like pains in the stomach, or feeling the beating of our heart), or sights. These are the sense-experiences that give us our most basic knowledge of the world.

What I have said about thoughts is also true of sense-experiences—that is to say, they are not to be found in the physical brain. They depend on the brain, and they come to us through our ears, mouths, skin, internal bodily organs, and eyes. But they are *more than physical*.

We can see this by looking at what modern physics says about the senses. Take the sense of sight, what we see with our eyes. In general, we see, among other things, what appear to be mostly colored, three-dimensional objects. But the most widely held account of the matter is that, first of all, colors do not exist if nobody is looking at them. Color, in the purely physical world, is a specific wavelength of light, somewhere between the infra-red and the ultra-violet. Some physicists believe that these wavelengths exist in about eleven dimensions. When such a wave (which is somehow also a particle, according to physicists, but that is another story) hits the eye, it imprints a two-dimensional image on the retina, which causes a set of electrical messages that pass to a number of different regions of the brain, and they cooperate to produce the sensation of a specific color.

The color is constructed by the apparatus of the bodily receptors and the brain. It does not exist in the outside world, since electro-magnetic waves have no color. Nor does it exist in the physical brain, because no observation ever finds colors in the gooey pinky-grey mass that is the brain.

Where, then, does the sensation of color exist? Well, it exists in the same place as thoughts, *in the mind*. And where is the mind? The strange truth is that it exists *no-where*. That is to say, it does not exist anywhere in space.

3. DREAMING

What I have just said may sound strange. And yet it is something we are very familiar with in our own experience (most of us, anyway). When we dream, we often seem to see ourselves in Romantic locations like the Bahamas. We see ourselves walking around or lying on a beach. We do very peculiar things, and impossible things happen all the time. Dreams do not obey the ordinary laws of nature. They are driven by imagination and often repressed fears and desires. But dreams happen. They exist. We "see" them. Some people see them in color. We have to ask people if they do, for we can never see other people's dreams. And we just have to believe what they say, because there is no way of checking whether they are right.

That is because dreams are not in any "real," physical world, with its laws of cause and effect, which anyone might observe if they look carefully. We might say they are "in our heads," but of course we do not mean that literally. If someone cuts our head open, no dreams are to be found.

Dreams happen in a sort of private inner space. We see things—bodies, beaches, and sea—that have a spatial relation to each other. The beach is next to the sea, and our body lies on top of the beach. That is a sort of spatial relationship. But dreams are not in any ordinary space. We cannot walk out of the beach and into our bedrooms. Dreams are, of course, in our minds, in a private space of our own, that nobody else can get into, and that has no spatial relation to our everyday world.

Other things exist in that private space. There are mental images—we can picture to ourselves all sort of places, real and imaginary. Many people also have sound-spaces. They can hear whole symphonies "in their heads." Perhaps dogs have smelly spaces. Fish might have watery spaces, for all we know, though they would perhaps all be wet dreams.

What are the experiences—the sounds and sights and smells—in these spaces made of? They do not seem to be made of matter, whether matter is a lot of solid lumps with mass and position or a set of waves in multi-dimensional space. They are simply sights, sounds, touches, smells, tastes, and sensations. They are not composed of smaller parts. They seem to be fundamental and elementary units that cannot be analyzed in any other way. Some philosophers have called them *qualia*; others call them *sense-data*.

Physical things can be broken down into molecules, atoms, and even smaller sub-atomic particles. They can all be observed by many people. They can often be measured, and their behavior can be confidently predicted by appeal to general laws of nature, which can be put into mathematical formulae.

Our sensory data do not seem to be like that. A note of music that we hear is just what it is. It may have pitch, timbre, amplitude, and perhaps direction (that is not very clear). But it is not made up of smaller elements.

So, if we ask what the real world is made of, what its basic constituents are, we have to say that for the physical world the basic constituents are quarks or electrons and so on (the physicist Carlo Rovelli says, "the world is made entirely from quantum fields"), together with some laws of nature. But we have to add that there are also elementary sensory data, which exist in various sets, which are each only observable by one person (the one who experiences them), and which do not exist at all when they are not being observed. They are parts of reality, but they are not parts of the physical world.

> *Sit and attend closely to what you are aware of. There are sounds, smells, perhaps tastes, certainly sights, bodily sensations, and tactile feelings (the slight pressure of a chair on your body, for instance). They are in constant change. They are your experiences, and nobody else can be aware of them in the way that you are. They make up your inner, private, world. This is true, and you know it to be true before you know anything about science or about how the brain works. It is the primary basis of all human knowledge.*

Each sense has its own private space. Fortunately, they all usually correlate with each other, though things can sometimes go wrong. Despite occasional discord, normally, bodily sensations, touches, sounds, smells, tastes, and sights all seem to harmonize with each other. We *hear* a sound and turn around to *see* what caused it, and move towards an object until we are able to *touch* it. All these different senses are involved in such a seemingly simple action, and each of them has its own special "space," the place in our minds that nobody else can get into, and that only we really know about.

In the case of humans, the senses of bodily sensation, touch, and sight are the most important. Among all the things we see, there is one thing that always seems to be present. That is, the observed body. It seems to be always there, often lurking in the background, wherever we are. This body has eyes, and it soon becomes obvious to us that whatever we see, we see from our eyes. If we close our eyes (or if we are blind), all sights disappear. The body, and specifically our eyes, give us a specific viewpoint from which we see the world of objects.

These viewpoints (in the case of seeing, we can call them "visual fields"; there are also touch-fields, sound-fields, and even smell-fields) differ slightly between different people. Nobody else ever has exactly the same viewpoint we have. That is just another way of saying that our visual experience is "private," and cannot be exactly shared with anyone else.

Of course, we do think there are other people with bodies and eyes. We see them, after all. But our body is special to us. If we look at it, we see arms and legs, which we can, to some extent, move. We can walk, and pick things up. We can open or close our eyes. We can stare hard at something or ignore it. Our body is the only part of our visual field over which we have, or seem to have, physical control.

Such efforts to exert control over parts of our body are an essential part of our experience. They affect the sort of experiences we have. For instance, if we concentrate hard on something, it appears quite different than it does if we just allow it to be a background that we are hardly aware of.

These efforts are intentions to do something. They may not always succeed, but at least we have a clear sense of trying to bring about some change in our bodies. That is an important part of our experience, too.

4. FREEDOM AND CREATIVITY

Some neuroscientists, who specialize in the study of the brain, are suspicious about the existence of a special sort of mental causality, of what is often called *free will*. They have a "bottom-up" view of the brain. That is, everything that happens in the brain is ultimately caused by the movements of sub-atomic particles, which obey the laws of physics. Those movements can, in principle, be explained purely by appeal to the basic laws of physics, and the nature of the fundamental particles themselves. They say that there is no need to appeal to some supra-physical reality—"the human will"—which interferes in that physical process by causing events to occur.

When I raise my arm, materialists argue, that act can be wholly explained by movements of muscles, caused by electrical impulses from the brain, which in turn are explained by the interaction of millions of neurons, all obeying the basic laws of nature. There is no room for an extra, non-physical, act of will, which could adjust the actions of those neurons to make my arm go up.

This theory is far beyond the possibility of proof, at least with the methods of modern science. It is a matter of *faith*—of belief going well beyond the evidence—that a *purely* physical explanation of human choices can be given. That faith is often driven by a firm commitment to materialism—that only material things exist. There are no spiritual things, no minds or non-material entities.

This faith is of course the opposite of the claim that minds—non-material things, or at least sets of non-material properties—are actually the things we are most sure of. Ordinary human experience tells us that, if we are fit, we can move our arms when we want to, and put them down again, even if we have no idea of what our neurons are doing, or even if we do not know that we have any neurons.

This seems to be a case of the testimony of experience versus a huge and not well-established generalization from a much more limited theory that physical events in the brain do cause observable behavioral effects.

For example, in a series of experiments at Harvard, Professor Pascual-Leone asked subjects to decide whether to raise either their right or their left hands, but to wait to implement their decision until they saw a green light. He then used magnetic stimulation of the motor cortex in the brain to cause people to raise one of their hands. What happened was that the hand selected by the motor cortex rose, whatever the subjects had previously decided. But in many cases, the subjects still said that they had acted voluntarily, and had perhaps changed their decision at the last moment. This seems to show that what may seem to be voluntary decisions may in fact be caused by physical events in the brain.

In another famous series of experiments initiated by the psychologist Benjamin Libet, it can be shown that the brain gets ready (it shows a "readiness potential") to raise a finger micro-seconds before the owner of the brain makes a conscious decision to do so. This too can be taken to imply that decisions—acts of will—are in fact rationalizations of events that the physical brain has *already* caused to happen. We think we are making a difference, but we are just being manipulated by our brains.

Before making the huge generalization that this is what always happens, however, we need to consider at least three things (apart from the many technical criticisms that have been made of the experiments in the professional journals). First of all, when such experiments are carried out, people are put into very artificial situations. They are seated in chairs, electrodes are placed on their skulls, and they are closely observed by scientists. This is not an ordinary life situation.

Second, what they are asked to do—raise a hand or finger—is something that has no moral, life-threatening, or vitally important consequences. It does not matter to them when they decide to move. The decision is completely arbitrary.

Third, the actions in question are the sorts of action that often happen involuntarily or unconsciously. Hands and fingers quite often twitch on their own, just as the heart beats on its own or blood flows through our veins without our being conscious of it. If I am asked to raise my finger at an arbitrary time, and my finger begins to twitch on its own, I might as well just agree with my finger, go with the flow, and say that is when I decided to raise it anyway. Or if I decide to raise my right hand, and my left hand begins to rise, I may just say that I changed my mind at the last moment. In such an artificial and arbitrary situation, the difference between my willing an act and my assenting to an act which has arisen subconsciously can be vanishingly small.

The really important decisions in human life are things like deciding whether to kill someone who threatens me, or whether to carry out an unpleasant duty when I do not have to do so. We are probably not attached to electrodes or seated in a chair at such times, so all that the experiments really show is that when things do not much matter, and when we know we are being experimented on, we would probably not override whatever physically caused events occurred in our bodies. It is significant that Dr. Libet himself has written that he does believe in free will, and he thinks that acts of will could override physically caused actions if it was important to do so.

The importance of having freedom from determination by brain-events is very great. When we hold people responsible for their actions, reward them for being good or punish them for being bad, we assume that they could have done other than they did. If one thing that gives meaning to life is the difficult endeavor to bring about a good result, this is because such endeavor is the result of personal effort, an effort that many people might not make. All our notions of creativity, heroism, and persistence, as well as of destructiveness, cowardice, and weakness, would collapse if we did not hold people responsible for their actions. We could hardly hold them responsible if they were determined to act as they did by their neurons, and so could never have done otherwise.

Suppose I form the intention of being kind to someone I dislike. I may have to struggle against my feelings of dislike, and force myself to be kind. Whatever actually causes my action, it is important that I consciously resolve what to do, persist in doing it, and conquer many of my feelings, however difficult that is. This resolve to make an effort is one of the most valued features of human action. To say that I cannot help doing what I do, because my brain is determining my action, would undermine my resolve.

If my beliefs are shown by my actions (whatever I might say theoretically) then my practical commitment shows that I believe my efforts are an essential causal factor in determining what happens. This belief is so strong that it would take an almost conclusive proof that I am not creatively free to make us give it up. There is no such conclusive proof. There is just a faith-commitment to materialism. And if there really are in the mind non-physical entities, properties, and purposive causes, materialism is almost certainly false. Human creativity and freedom, human purpose and intention, are fundamental features of human experience and knowledge.

5. THE SELF AS AGENT

There are many factors that contribute to human action. People may decide how much they will be influenced by the ideals and values that they may (correctly) feel to be objective features of reality. They may decide how much they will be influenced by the varied experiences they have had, and how they have responded to those experiences in the past. They may decide how much they will be influenced by the diverse behavior-patterns rooted in the structure of the brain, which often operate at an unconscious level, and may well conflict with each other. And they may decide how much they will be influenced by the people they know and trust, and by the social context in which they live. In any decision, there are multiple influencing factors to be considered, and it would be unwise to neglect any of them.

None of these factors are completely determining. That is to say, they do not cause one specific future, excluding all other possibilities. There are a number of different possible futures on each occasion of action. Quantum theory seems to force us to allow that events are not wholly determined, but may follow any of a number of possible paths into the future (see the Appendix). If this is true, the future is to some extent open. This suggests that the mind may be influenced by many causal factors in a given situation, but that influence will not force it to make one predetermined choice. The choice it makes is what will decide its future, and the future of that part of the world in which it exists.

Sometimes people say that a rational mind will always decide what it thinks is best. Perhaps this is so; but we need to ask "best *for whom*?" It can decide what is best for itself in the present situation, or what is best for the increase of objective value in the world. This is the fundamental choice facing human beings. Nothing determines that choice but the deciding mind itself, which thereby creates what it will in future be.

It is important to recognize that there are many factors that may make such decisions difficult, or sometimes impossible. Those who believe in human freedom do not say that humans are totally free on all occasions. They only need to say that in *some* critical situations, humans possess *some degree* of freedom, but it is probably impossible for anyone, whether themselves or others, to be sure what that degree is. For that reason, it is wise not to be too hasty in judging the actions of others, even though a general belief in human freedom is a basic foundation of our relationships in human society.

There are some neuroscientists who say that human thoughts are nothing more than patterns of electrical activity in our brains, and that therefore the sense of a continuing and responsible self is an illusion. There are even books with titles like, *The Illusion of the Self*. Since such books are freely and creatively written, I can hardly disapprove of them! But I do think they are grossly misleading. The sense of self is one of the distinguishing marks of human mentality, and to lack it—not to know that you are responsible for your past actions, or that you can to some extent shape your own future—is to be in need of medical assistance.

There is no reason to disagree with neuroscientists when they point out that what physically happens in the brain is that there are spreading patterns of electrical activity among billions of neurons, patterns that are continually being either built up or inhibited as life progresses. When those patterns are disrupted or destroyed, conscious experiences, memories, and thoughts are also disrupted or destroyed. In that sense, *the mind depends on the brain*. That means that the correct functioning of the brain is a necessary condition of being a fully developed human person. But it does not mean that there is nothing more to being a proper person than having a functioning brain. That would be like saying that because breathing oxygen is a necessary condition of being alive, life is nothing more than breathing oxygen. The argument is clearly absurd.

What more is needed for someone to be a morally responsible person? In English law, you are not responsible unless:

1. you know what you are doing

2. you know if it is right or wrong, and

3. you could have done otherwise.

I think this is correct. It supposes that you have a sense that you are a continuing self. You know that you are the same person who acted freely in the past, and that your actions back then deserve a punishment or a reward now.

If the self is an illusion, this would not be true. Without a "self" the whole idea of "desert"—that if you work hard, you deserve some sort of reward, and if you neglect your duties, you should be punished—would disappear.

There can be no doubt that there is a unity of consciousness, which ensures that a whole set of sensory data—sights, sounds, feels, smells, and tastes—cohere in one total experience to which only one person has direct access. This unity also extends temporally, so that, in standard cases, memories of past experiences and expectations of future experiences also belong to one privately accessible chain of consciousness.

Moreover, actions that you performed in the past have consequences for you in the present and future. You can distinguish, with varying degrees of clarity, things that you are responsible for (like working hard for an exam, and so getting a good mark) and things you are not responsible for (like being shot by a criminal). You are the same agent now that you were then.

What the idea of the "self" does is to point to the unique access there is to one set of thoughts, feelings, and perceptions, and to the continuing, if limited, responsibility there is for creating future states and events. The self is what has such unique access and responsibility. It is the continuing "you."

When some philosophically minded neurologists speak of a "self," they are often thinking of some specific mechanism in the brain that controls what happens. It will be located somewhere in the brain and will be an essential and unchanging core that remains the same while all experiences, thoughts, and intentions change. They then are apt to deny that such a self exists. And they are right. But that is *not* what the self is.

It is better to take a much more holistic view, and consider the self as the totality of mental, bodily, and social interactions that constitute a human person. The self is not a particular member of a series, whether the series is bodily or mental. The self is not something that never changes, something that remains the same underneath all its different thoughts and feelings. *The self is the continually changing and developing totality of the series.* Or it may be better to say that it is what holds together huge amounts of different data as members of one consciousness, and what acts creatively within one successive chain of consciousness to shape its future.

What makes "free" decisions is not a part of the mind, even less is it part of the physical brain. It is a whole constituted of one unique mind and brain, within a unique social and environmental context. That whole receives stimuli from its world, and creatively responds in a way influenced but not wholly determined by past experiences, inbuilt behavior-patterns, social relationships, and apprehensions of objectively existing values.

This thought should not be alien even to materialist thinkers, for they commonly assert that it is "the brain as a whole" that comes to decisions. All I am asserting is that "the whole" should also include, as well as physical brain-events, both mental contents and social context. This will help to explain how we can seem to be different persons in different social contexts, or when some brain-processes predominate over others, or when we are in different emotional moods. The sense in which we remain the same is the sense in which this chain of experiences—this body, this brain, and this social and historical context—is not literally shared by any others, and in which at least the most fundamental decisions of this total person are freely and responsibly made.

6. THE SENSORY WORLD

I have spoken mostly about the senses of sight, touch, bodily sensation, and the sense we have of acting creatively and responsibly. There is another factor of experience that is very important. That is the factor of feeling and of evaluation. The senses of touch and bodily sensation, in particular, can have the property of being pleasant or of being painful. Our visual field we may find attractive or repelling, but such feelings are not usually very intense. Bodily sensations, however, can be extremely painful or pleasant, ranging from excruciating pain to physical ecstasy. If anything touches the surface of our body (the skin) we feel it. Inside our skin, we also feel many sensations—the heart beating, the stomach rumbling, a tooth aching.

These sensations seem to have a life of their own. The heart beats whether we feel it or not, and we can rarely control it. Some sensations, however, we have some control over. We can take action to extract an aching tooth or take medicine to ease a muscular pain.

No one else can know or have my pain. People may say "I feel your pain," but they just mean they can sympathize with us. If we could literally feel the pain of others, visiting the sick would become an unbearably painful experience. I cannot normally, and most us can never, move things outside our own bodies, however hard we try. That seems to be a privilege of gods or great saints, and there are not many of them. I never feel pains in other physical objects than myself. I have never heard anyone say, "I have a pain in my bicycle."

Many other feelings exist in addition to the simple bodily feelings of pleasure and pain. But those simple feelings, while they undoubtedly exist, are not properties of the physical world. Bicycles do not have pains. People have pains, and many other feelings too, and they are only experienced by the people who have them. The world of feelings is a private world, and it introduces the element of value into reality. I do not value pain, but I do value pleasure. I seek to experience things I value, and to avoid things that give me pain or distress. Feelings are reactions to what is experienced. Such reactions exist, but only in minds. They give rise to responsive actions that cause objective changes in the world. Because of their close relation to sensory perceptions, they help to emphasize the point that what minds perceive is not just what objectively exists. It is already colored by an element of personal interpretation and response. We do not sense neutral data in a wholly passive way. Our perceptions of reality embody and express a uniquely personal and active reaction to what exists.

The senses of sight, touch, and sensation seem to be of most importance for evoking our feeling responses to the world. The other main senses—of sounds, tastes, and smells—are less important to most of us, though they too can evoke feelings that can be very powerful. There is a sort of sound-space. We can hear many different sounds at the same time. But we do not really relate them spatially to each other. However, we do tend to locate sounds in space—to the right or left of us, near or far away. That is probably because we hear with our ears, and we locate ears at a particular point in visual and tactile space, on each side of the head. We can locate sounds by turning our heads and by seeing what observable things in visual space might be producing those sounds.

We might hear sounds that do not come from our ears— sounds "in the head." Many musicians can do that. We then cannot locate the sounds anywhere. Like the mental images that most of us have from time to time, they are in a "space" of their own. But they usually are still derived from sounds that we have heard with our ears, and in that way they are still connected with the idea of a "real world" in which we are embodied.

Similarly, we locate tastes in or around our mouths. But that is because we see the food or liquid we put in our mouths and feel it swishing about inside us. We now know that if we stimulate the appropriate part of the brain electrically, we could have some sort of taste. So, when we "place" tastes in our mouths we are in fact relating them causally to parts of our visual and tactile spaces.

As for smells, dogs do seem to be aware of very interesting smelly spaces. We are not, and again we locate smells in our noses, because it is when we sniff that we get a smell. But the fact is that smells are not physically inside our noses at all. Noses are just parts of a complicated chain of electrical impulses to the brain that somehow cause smells to pop up in our minds.

All our sensations—visual, tactile, bodily, aural, smelly, and tasty—are closely integrated, largely by being centered on one body, which is part of a wider reality, represented internally to one experiencing mind.

All these sensations are private. What we experience by means of the senses is never completely shared with anyone else. It can be pleasant or unpleasant. And we can partly influence what we experience by moving parts of our body.

We really are embodied in the world. The body grows and decays; the heart beats and stops; we move around in an environment that, for the most part, we do not choose or control. Yet we have private perceptions of that world, more or less intense feelings about it, and more or less limited intentional attempts to influence our perceptions and feelings. So if we ask what we really are, as human beings, we should say that we are physical bodies in a real public world, but that is not *all* we are, and it is not even the most important thing about us. What is really important is our private perceptions, feelings, thoughts, and intentions. This is the world of our minds, a world of experiences and thoughts that really exists and is not just reducible to the physical things that the natural sciences talk about.

7. VALUE AND PURPOSE

One big difference between the world of personal experience and the physical world the natural sciences talk about is that in our experience-world we often do things in order to achieve some purposes that we have. We might think of football, and decide to try to become a good footballer. Then we might practice in order to achieve that goal. We have purposes, things that we value, that we think are good. And we act in order to achieve those purposes.

This is one of the most obvious things about human life. We act in order to reach some goal that we value and set for ourselves, or maybe to avoid something that we think will give us pain. We are agents with purposes. Yet values and purposes do not seem to exist in the world as known by the natural sciences. Physicists have long ago stopped asking what the purpose of the law of gravity is, and they do not, when they are doing physics, have to decide whether or not gravity is a good thing. Yet purpose and value are major features of our internal experience-world. They help to mark the difference between the public world with which the sciences deal and the private worlds of human experience.

Our sense that some things are good and some are bad probably begins with the obvious fact that bodily sensations can be either pleasant (good) or painful (bad). But feelings of good and bad extend well beyond that. I can feel happy (good) or depressed (bad), excited (good) or remorseful (bad), sympathetic (good) or callous (bad). These are all feelings, states that I know by acquaintance, and no one else can know my feelings in the same way that I do. They are not, however, bodily sensations. They cannot be located in my body, as pains can be. They are in the mind.

When we are in pain, we cry out and maybe jump around. When we are excited, we do the same sort of thing, but in a rather different way. There is usually some typical behavior, which other people can see, that expresses our mental feelings, which other people cannot see.

But that close link does not always exist. As any good actor will tell you, you can feign crying or laughing behavior when you are not sad or happy, so the behavior is not straightforwardly identical with felt sorrow or joy.

It does not seem right to say that such behavior is just an effect of bodily feelings. The relationship seems closer than that. It rather seems that the behavior and the feeling are two aspects of the same thing. Only one aspect is observable by others—more precisely, others observe a body very much like the one we observe, but from a slightly different viewpoint. That aspect, the behavior, can by a special effort be either feigned or suppressed. If that happens, other people cannot be sure if we are really in pain or happy. Yet suppressing behavior does take a special effort, and the two aspects normally go together. There is a natural and regular connection, but not a necessary one.

At this point you may want to say that this is just to state the obvious, that we exist as persons in a community of persons. We know each other primarily through our behavior, but we each have thoughts and feelings that we need never disclose to others.

That is true. But we do not always take seriously enough the fact that all knowledge begins from human experience, and human experience is primarily of a world of interacting, sometimes competing and sometimes cooperating, values, purposes, and meanings. Any view of human existence that denies, ignores, or down-plays these facts is not giving an adequate account of human existence.

8. THOUGHTS

As I have noted, many human feelings are more closely linked with thoughts than with behavior or with bodily sensations. Feelings like a sense of anticipation are not literally in the body, though they often have bodily sensations associated with them. They may be expressed in trembling or "jumping about" behavior. But they do not *have* to be. Yet they do essentially seem to presuppose the existence of relevant *thoughts*.

Anticipation, for instance, involves *thinking* of some state as (i) in a reasonably near future, (ii) as pleasing, and (iii) as attainable. Without those thoughts, anticipation would not exist.

I can choose to dwell on the thoughts, picture the future events, and even begin to have a foretaste of the pleasure I will take in them. To some extent I can control my thoughts, concentrating on them or putting them aside, though much of the time what I think about will generate feelings that I cannot control. If I lose someone I love, I may not be able to stop thinking about him or her, and feeling sad.

Thought and feeling are closely associated. They both ultimately depend on the occurrence of perceptions, but they are much more than perceptions, and they may move so far beyond perceptions—like the feeling of guilt for having done something believed to be wrong, or like the thoughts we have when doing pure mathematics—that they seem to lose contact with the sensory world altogether.

We must add feelings and thoughts to the inventory of things in our experience-world, in addition to perceptions, sensations, and intentions. Feelings and thoughts are like a continually changing series of states or events in the non-spatial reality of the mind.

It is thought that interprets our experience, moderates our feelings, and formulates our intentions. It is reasonable to think that many animals interpret their experience, have feelings, and aim to achieve goals. But human thoughts are distinctive because they are typically expressed in language. When we think, we think in words that we have learned from others in a particular society.

The exact symbols used in a language—its words—are not usually of great significance in and of themselves. What is important is what they *mean*.

Knowing what a word means is not a matter of having particular perceptions, mental images, or feelings to which thoughts refer. It is being able to understand a concept, a quite distinctive mental activity that has to be learned, and an activity at which some people are much better than others.

Language determines what kinds of things are picked out in a specific society, or what kinds of activity are valued or abhorred. When we understand words, we understand how our experiences are divided up, and how we are to feel and act in response to the experienced world.

Languages are not fixed and unchanging. They change in response to new experiences. While formulated in language, thoughts are general concepts that the language we have learned may not express well. Language can be extended and improved, as we search for terms that will seem more adequate to our understanding. We are not imprisoned in the language we have learned, but neither are we free to think without that language. What we can do is deal creatively with language as we meet new experiences, so that our thinking is a continual interaction between experience, interpretation, and changing understanding.

Words are not confined to describing actual events. They can be used to describe imagined worlds. Words lead us to think of things that are possible, not just actual. They introduce us to worlds of possibility. Once we can imagine possible worlds, we are well on the way to doing pure mathematics. For mathematics is the construction of possible worlds that may have lost any connection with our perceived world.

One great pure mathematician, G. H. Hardy, said that his aim was to construct a mathematical system that had no possible use in the real world. Unfortunately for him, his work did later prove very useful in genetics and quantum physics. I do not suppose this would really have disappointed him, but he would still, I think, have preferred the intrinsic beauty of his equations to the uses to which they were put. There is something beautiful about pure mathematical thought, and it is as far from sensory experience as humans can hope to get.

This shows that imagining possibilities is not just fantasy. It can be the doorway to a greater understanding of reality. Pure thought-experiments led Einstein to the theory of relativity, and to the discovery of quantum entanglement by George Bell. Words can become vehicles of exploration and investigation; they enable us to build large-scale theories, even about the beginning and end of our universe.

Thoughts, even though they are usually expressed by means of words and language that we have learned from our own social networks, can take us far beyond present experience and our immediate reactions to it. They can give an understanding of the nature of existence itself.

It is thought that enables us to interpret apparently subjective human perceptions as the experience of an objective world and of personal beings within that world with whom we interact. From other persons, we learn to be creative, to create sounds, colors, words, tastes, and smells that are attractive. We do not do this just to please ourselves. We are trying to create something that can be appreciated by others. As we receive our experiences from a reality outside of ourselves, so we seek to create states that are not part of ourselves, and that can be perceived by others. We learn this largely by observing and imitating the behavior of others, by valuing what they do and trying to do the same ourselves. We cooperate with others to bring about new states of affairs, and we try to help them when they seem to need help.

This means that we are essentially *other-oriented* beings, receiving, shaping, and contributing as parts of an ever-changing communal process of realizing new shared values and purposes. We do not have a problem of escaping from our private and self-contained little worlds of perception. Our perceptions, though unique to us, are perceptions of a world that is given to, and can be interpreted and shaped by, many creative and responsive agents.

Human beings are not just very complicated physical objects in one public three-dimensional space, which may have some peripheral and purely subjective features (minds), that have no real causal effects in the world. On the contrary, a human being is primarily a complex of precisely correlated private spaces. The contents of these spaces are interpreted using notions of value (what we like or dislike), purpose (what we try to get or avoid), and personal relationship (intentional interaction) that have little or no place in purely physical descriptions of the world. In the universe as it is described by physics, there are no values, no purposes, and no intentional actions. There are just value-free laws that are not trying to aim at anything at all.

Human private spaces contain perceptions, feelings (reactions), and thoughts (interpretations of sensory perceptions as "of" something, and active responses to it). Together, they constitute a "life-world" that is unique to each individual. Each set of experiences leaves memory traces and confirms or weakens inborn dispositional feelings and responsive behaviors.

In our life-worlds we respond to the reality we perceive, taking it to include, most importantly to us, a response to other centers of experience and intentional action. Major parts of the objective reality we perceive are taken to be personal. That is, those parts—the constantly changing human bodies that interact with us—are seen as being aware of us, taking an interest in us, and responding to what we do. Our response is not to some disinterested succession of perceptions. It is to a reality much of which is seen as expressed in interactive, creative, and responsive behavior.

The personal here transcends the purely physical. The observed behavior of other bodies is interpreted as an expression of thoughts and experiences, and a response to our expressed thoughts and experiences. In mutual creativity and responsiveness, human experience takes on a new dimension. This dimension is essentially *expressed* in and through the physical. Yet to reduce it to the physical, whether in dispassionately observable behavior or in some physical activity in the brain, is to miss its real nature.

This is a key difference between a scientific approach to nature and a personal, experience-centered, approach. A scientific approach abstracts from any elements of real creativity in nature—events are determined by laws of nature, and are not oriented towards any goal or purpose. A scientific approach abstracts from any idea of states that are of value for their own sake, and are chosen to exist for that reason—there is no conscious choice in sub-atomic physics, and no purpose in the mutation of genetic material. And a purely scientific approach abstracts from ideas of a relationship between entities that is more than an exchange of physical properties. Hard science does not speak of love, of duty, of aesthetic appreciation, or of friendship, even though these things are the heart and reality of human existence.

The scientific approach is invaluable and has changed our understanding of nature. It is by no means to be ignored or opposed. Yet for any adequate understanding of human nature, it must be regarded as *incomplete*. A place has to be found for the life-worlds of sensation, perception, feeling, and thought, for value, meaning, and purpose; in short, for the existence of mind.

9. MIND AND OBJECTIVE REALITY

The mental world is a rich and complex world. It includes perceived data, reactive feeling, conceptual understanding, imaginative generalization, and formulations of possible active responses to achieve some valued goal. The mind is identified, not by having some spatial position, as physical bodies are, but by its contents, which are unique to each individual. The body stands to the mind as the provider of data and the vehicle of purposive change. The mind exists and is from the first experienced as a member of a community of minds, from which it learns and with which it interacts. These minds exist at various stages of intimacy and capacity—in animals as well as humans.

On this view, mind is primary, and the world is what enables minds to gain knowledge, to interact, and to create and pursue new values. Understanding, value, and purpose are irreducible realities, known to us immediately and by acquaintance. The purely physical world, as it is conceived by the natural sciences, is an inference and abstraction, a construction of human thought, derived from our experience.

That does not mean the world is not real. There can be little doubt that our body puts us in touch with a reality beyond our perceptions of it. The sense-organs, the central nervous system, and the brain cause our perceptions to be what they are. Our bodies generate a perception-world that does attempt to represent external reality. My point is that this perception-world is different from the reality it represents. I shall argue in the next part that the objective physical world is itself an expression of mind, in this case a supreme Mind, and could not exist without that Mind.

All I am arguing at present, however, is that what we experience—the experience itself—is different from the objective reality that causes the experiences. Our sights and sounds are not in themselves objective. They come and go, are more or less clear and intense, and give particular viewpoints from within a wider reality that is independent of us.

Quite a lot of our lives is largely or sometimes completely unconscious. Some sorts of mental events occur without us even being aware of them. Consciousness varies a lot in intensity. We may be unaware of our surroundings, or we might attend closely to them. Some people are much more observant than others. I can go into a room, and obviously in some sense I see what is there. Yet I might be quite unable to say how many panes of glass there are in the windows, unless I look more carefully at what is there in my field of vision.

In the mind, there is a spectrum from complete unawareness to careful inspection. This shows that we cannot identify our consciousness of objects with the objects as they exist in themselves. Conscious perceptions are real; but they are clearly different from the objects we perceive, which we may perceive truly or falsely, accurately or inaccurately, clearly or obscurely.

Because of this, our sensory experiences are naturally and immediately taken to be "of" a reality that we do not experience as it is in itself. We could say that our sensory experiences are signs or subjective impressions of an objective world (by which I mean, a world that exists apart from our perceptions of it). They represent that world via a particular array of physical sense-organs, a nervous system, and a brain in a particular body. What they give us is not usually false or illusory, though it can be sometimes. But it is different in kind and feel from what objectively exists.

Our bodies, of course, are parts of this objective reality, though what we perceive of the body is a representational image too. That image, or complex of images, is in the mind. It is common to think that our minds are in our bodies. Odd as it may sound at first, our bodies—more exactly, our bodies *as they are perceived and known by us*—are in our minds.

That does not mean there is no external reality. It does mean, however, that external reality, as it is when it is not being perceived, is not the same as what we perceive. What you see is not what there really is.

10. ARTIFICIAL INTELLIGENCE

With the extraordinary expansion of computer technology and artificial intelligence, it is often said that computers could do all the things that we do, and that we can explain this without reference to minds or mental contents. But is this really true?

Computers and thinking machines can be programmed to play chess and conduct apparently sensible conversations. They can recognize faces, or they can remember and play songs and symphonies. Yet we know that all that is going on inside a computer is a huge series of on/off switches, processing a series of binary numbers. On a CD, for instance, a series of o's and 1's stands for a specific note of music. But that series is not a sound. It is a code that, given the right equipment, can cause a sound. The sound has been turned into a set of binary numbers, which have to be turned back into a sound by a device constructed for that purpose. When you say that the numbers represent a sound, you really mean that the numbers can, given the proper equipment, be decoded to produce a sound, which humans, but not computers, can hear. All the work done by the computer can be described in purely physical terms.

What computers do not have is the perceptions and feelings that in the human case are the referents of verbal symbols. A machine can detect and respond with a pre-set response to a specific set of data. Advanced computers can learn and develop new strategies, within limits set by human designers. But they lack any perceptions of and feelings about those data, and they have no intentions with regard to them. They have no "private space" in which perceptions, feelings, and intentions could occur. They are automata, with no inner life, nothing that is valued for its own sake, and nothing that takes concentration and effort to achieve.

By contrast, because perceptions, feelings, thoughts, and intentions exist, human thought cannot be analyzed without remainder into sets of physical properties.

Consider the question, "Is the existence of a computer worthwhile?" It may be worthwhile *to us*, if it makes our work easier, but *it* cannot know it is worthwhile, or put any value on its existence, or pursue any purposes of its own. Humans are special precisely because they can ask what is valuable about their existence and can set themselves to pursue things that they find to be of value.

11. THE IRONY OF MATERIALISM

Sometimes people say that they think "in their heads," as if thoughts were electrical process in the brain. We do not always see how unusual this perspective is. The ancient Greeks believed that they thought with their stomachs, and that brains were some sort of air-conditioning unit for cooling the blood. It is relatively recently in human history that people have realized that brains are necessary for thinking, and that they are not very good for air-conditioning.

We now know quite a lot about brains. We can locate which parts of the brain are active when people think. We can even tell what sorts of things, in general, people are thinking about or experiencing by examining the chemical and electrical activity in part of the brain. But it is not true that we can "see people's thoughts." What we can see is what must be operating in the physical brain if people are to have thoughts. If we want to know what people are thinking about, we have to ask the owners of brains exactly what thoughts they are having. And then we just have to believe them.

It is ironic that the picture of the world as it is painted by some modern scientists (not all, by any means), is a picture of a purely material world without purpose, value, or meaning, ruled by universal unconscious laws. Yet that picture is in fact a pure thought-construction, dependent on the development of mathematical models that involve such things as imaginary numbers and highly imaginative hypotheses (like positing eleven dimensions, or vibrating strings in one dimension, or alternative universes that all exist alongside each other).

Modern physics requires a grasp of higher mathematics, and the ability to imagine possibilities from a new and different point of view. This is above all a world of abstract thought and active enquiry.

To say that the universe is a self-contained world of absolute, universal, and unbreakable laws is one product of such thought and enquiry. That model seems to many scientists to have broken down under the impact of quantum theory. Whether or not that is so, my point is that what the natural sciences involve is a high degree of active intellectual enquiry and theory-construction.

Theories need to be tested. But you have to have the theory before you can test it, and very few of us have the ability to construct such theories. To do so is to have a very sophisticated purpose or aim; one has to place a high value on intellectual understanding; and one has to use symbols that have meaning. The irony is that a highly purposive, valuable, and meaningful activity has to be engaged in to produce a theory that nature has no purposes, values, or meaning. Physicists are parts of nature, so at least parts of nature have purpose and value. This obvious fact stands in need of explanation.

Part Two

COSMOS

1. THE COSMIC MIND

ANY ACCURATE DESCRIPTION OF reality has to include minds as well as bodies, experience-worlds as well as a public objective world. These should not be thought of as two quite distinct worlds acting independently but correlated in some mysterious way.

If the real world is not known as it is in itself, there seem to be two main possible conceptions of its real nature. One is favored by large sections of the scientific community. It is that the objective world is a world of general laws, without purpose or value, but with amazing mathematical precision and beauty. The mental world is a product of this reality, but only a temporary and transient product, doomed to extinction, and having a brief and highly improbable existence in a tiny part of the universe. The weakness of this view is that the emergence of purpose and value and consciousness from a world totally without them is wholly mysterious, and there is no satisfying explanation of why the basic laws and constants of nature are as they are. Einstein and others appeal to necessity, but what could make basic laws necessary is unexplained, since our laws of nature seem to be a selection from many possible sets of laws. One could easily imagine the laws of nature being different from what they in fact are.

The other conception is that the objective world is mind-like in nature. It does have general laws of nature, but it also has values and purposes. The beauty of nature's fundamental laws is itself of value, and the physical world exists to produce value by a purpose-directed process of emergence. The weakness of this view is that there is so little consciousness in the universe, and the universe will in any case die out eventually. There is so much suffering in life that it is hard to see it as part of a valuable purpose. It would be a satisfying explanation of being that it is intrinsically worthwhile. That is a good reason for existing. But that there is a good reason for something does not make it exist. Unless, that is, there already exists a mind that acts for reasons; but why should *that* mind exist? And why is there so much *suffering*, if this mind acts for good reasons?

In face of these considerations, it seems to me that the most plausible option is one that takes something of each view into account. There does exist, as Einstein wished, a necessary being, a being that has to exist and have the general nature that it has. It is unlikely that this is just a particular set of laws of nature, because there are probably many such possible sets of laws.

Some quantum physicists have suggested that all possible worlds, all possible sets of laws, exist. These laws might be necessary, like the basic rules of mathematics (like 2+2=4). They just have to be the way they are. If you had a complete set of all possible mathematical laws, that set might have this sort of necessity.

Then you might realize that possible things cannot really exist, since they are not actual. But we do have one model for possible things existing. Minds can think of possible things; a mind could be an actual thing that contained, as its thoughts, all possible laws, states, and universes. These would not be actual, but they would not be just nothing. They would be possibilities, things that *could* exist. The cosmic mind (I will now call it "Mind" with a capital M, to distinguish it from minds that are generated within the cosmos) necessarily contains all possibilities, which are necessarily what they are.

That gives you necessity. But some things actually do exist. There must be some principle of selection, and some power that can bring them into existence. A cosmic Mind could do that. It knows all possible things, and so it knows which are good (which are worth existing) and which are bad (which are not worth existing). If it can, it will obviously choose good states. That is a rational principle of selection. But would it have the power to do so?

This is very hard to say, since we cannot know what is in the cosmic Mind, if it exists. But we can easily imagine that if there are lots of good states that are possible, any mind that could would bring them into being. At that point it may be wise to be a little bit agnostic about the power of the cosmic Mind. We should not be too quick to call it "omnipotent," as though it could do absolutely anything. After all, if it is necessarily what it is, it may have to do some things, whether it positively wants to or not.

There would be a positive reason to bring about good things. But maybe in bringing about good things, the cosmic Mind also *has* to bring about things that are negative or destructive possibilities. Maybe the creative possibilities for actual worlds that exist in its Mind are entangled with possibilities for destruction. Even the cosmic Mind cannot disentangle them, because they are *necessarily* interconnected, and one cannot exist without the other.

Observation of the actual world we have almost compels the conclusion that Mind (if there is one) brings about both good, creative, productive things and bad, destructive, and negative things. Mind originates life *and* death. The cosmos is a field of creation *and* destruction, cooperation *and* competition. However, it may be possible to forge life out of death, happiness out of suffering. The cosmos is a field of both good and bad, but insofar as it has a rational purpose it may be able to generate intrinsic values out of such a mixed beginning. The cosmos cannot produce good without evil, creation without destruction, synergy without alienation. The cosmos is in its origin both creative and destructive, but where rational choice exists, it must aim at the good.

The cosmic Mind, on this view, is a blend of necessity, chance, and reason. Creative and destructive powers emanate from a primordial Mind by necessity. Not everything is necessary, however. There is an openness (which at first appears as chance) in nature that allows creative purpose to exist. Those purposes are rational when they are directed to bringing about states and processes of value. This suggests that a cosmic Mind would seek to bring good out of evil, empower goodness, and eliminate evil as far as possible. The laws of the universe are "selected" because they can produce distinctive sorts of value. Embodied intelligent minds emerge, which can understand and use the laws to produce new values. These values become ideals, which form the rational purpose of the universe and of human existence.

2. CREATIVE CHANGE

We can get some idea of why even Mind could not choose a universe that contains nothing but good states. Good states like pleasure are parts of a continuum that extends from intense pleasure to intense pain, and many pleasures are mixed with some pain. For example, the pleasure of achieving a difficult goal could not exist without the relative pain caused by difficulties on the way to such achievement. It is possible that, for many people, those difficulties might not be overcome, which would entail the existence of another and probably greater sort of pain.

Again, if creative change is actual, that will often mean the destruction of the old. New life builds on the old, but if it is to be truly novel, it must take a different course from the old. It must transcend the old, and yet include elements of the old in a new form. Forces of reaction and conservation will vie with forces of reform and revolution. And those creative forces will themselves differ as they pursue their own creative paths. If many individual minds are freely creative, then conflicts will be virtually inevitable, as different goals are pursued that may frustrate each other.

In addition, if changes are truly creative, they will include attempts that are unsuccessful and experiments that fail. In that situation, some minds may cause pain to others, out of envy or pride, disappointment or desire to dominate. The existence of communities of creative minds will introduce specific forms of suffering or discontent into existence.

At the pre-mental level, the structure of being must prepare the way for such creative and relational communities. There must be predictable general laws that will enable minds to plan their futures. There must be open alternatives that will allow free creativity to develop. And there must be some creative power that causes the new to emerge from the old, a power not fully determining and yet pressing towards a genuinely emergent future.

Darwinian biologists often stress that the evolution of life is a struggle for survival. Survival is not, as such, however, an intrinsic value. It all depends on what sort of thing it is that survives. The struggle, in an emergentist view, is not just to survive, but to increase in value, especially to increase in creativity and in cooperative relationships with others.

The opposite of creativity is complete dependence on some other being, where no personal freedom at all is permitted. To be creative, a being must minimally be partly free from such external determination. But if that is all that exists, it amounts to little more than an element of randomness without reason. Creativity increases if there is a reason for taking one path or one set of paths rather than others.

A random choice of colors in a painting may be undetermined, but it is unlikely to form a beautiful or coherent pattern. What is needed is some sort of plan—to shape a pattern or paint a portrait, perhaps. The pattern can be shaped as the process continues; it does not have to be totally pre-formed in the mind. Action follows a pattern of its own making, taking possible paths that build up into a coherent or beautiful whole. Each step is undetermined, but there is a vector, a direction, towards beauty or coherence, which allows a number of choices but blocks those that threaten to destroy the forming pattern.

This is like artistic endeavor; one aims to form a pattern of some sort, not fully defined in advance. This is not at first a conscious choice. It is a process of pattern-formation, guided by archetypes of beauty, which allow variety but express order and harmony. Some moves will continue to be truly random, but there is a guiding power that ensures that order and harmony will be expressed overall. This guiding power is a function of the cosmic Mind, which in this aspect could be seen as the artist of being.

True creativity increases when conscious goals form, and one acts in order to attain them. It becomes fuller when we reflect on our ideals, when we respond to them as normative (good, true, and beautiful), and are consciously guided by our conception of an objective ideal that is filled out in detail during the process of creation. Such objective ideal goals are rooted in cosmic Mind.

As with creativity, so with personal relationship. The minimum of relationship is unconcern with the being of most others. We begin to relate positively to others when we form groups to defend against competitors. This can occur at pre-mental stages, when bodies build and protect themselves against attack. In animals, cooperation becomes conscious, and in humans it is experienced as an objective goal of action and feeling. Gradually we can extend our range of cooperation and concern. The ideal goals are to be shared by and extended to all beings, so far as possible.

The goal for humans is not to stay unchangingly in blissful contemplation of perfect beauty. That is perhaps the goal of a changelessly perfect being, a being whose goal is always and necessarily achieved, the 'Actus Purus' of medieval theology. The human goal is the attainment of happiness and fulfilment through the pursuit of virtue (excellence) in the face of difficulties and obstacles.

Where virtue exists as an intrinsic good, there must exist a real possibility of failing to attain virtue, and even of opposing the virtue that is found in others, which may wrongly appear as a threat to oneself. There will be the real possibility of killing, lying, the destruction of the environment, and the oppression and hatred of others. That means that the world in which virtue exists cannot be a world in which everything happens for the best. It will be a world that necessarily contains the possibility of conflict and warfare. It will be a world in which people can kill, lie, destroy, and oppress, seeking their own good at the expense of others. It will be a world in which the destructive possibilities of being, which have always been present, will be unleashed by human choices.

Such a world will be "open" in that it will have many points at which alternative futures are possible. It will not be wholly determined either by God or by alleged absolute laws of nature. Human conceptions of a possible future will have causal efficacy, so minds will have real, though limited, causal power. Since there are many minds, their purposes and actions can conflict, though they can also cooperate to achieve common goals.

It will be a world in which people have capacities that they must realize through work. It will be in need of shaping and ordering. It is not a world that is complete, perfect, and ordered to human requirements. It provides basic materials that need to be constructed, land that must be cultivated, cities that must be built, discoveries that need to be made. It is a field for creative and imaginative activity, potential for many projects. Humans are creators of order out of largely unformed or even obstructive material. That material will enable, but will also often frustrate, human actions. The world is to be formed by work.

3. MIND AND PURPOSE

Some have thought that minds, or spirits, exist apart from matter, and come to be embodied in matter for some reason, perhaps to experience sensual pleasure or novel forms of existence. The philosopher Plato thought that, and so have many Indian philosophers.

Aristotle, Plato's pupil, and one of the most influential of all philosophers, proposed that human minds, which he called "intellectual (or intelligent) souls," are minds capable of abstract thought and moral evaluation. They are not from some separate spiritual realm. They are one kind of soul (by a "soul" he meant something like a principle of life), distinguished by having intellectual capacities. There were animal souls, whose capacities were more limited, though they had awareness of their environment, and purposive behavior. He even proposed that there were vegetable souls, identified by their capacities to grow and reproduce.

For Aristotle, these different sorts of souls had different capacities, and they were associated with, and formed the essential natures (what he called the "forms"), of various sorts of physical bodies—plants, animals, and humans.

It was not until the nineteenth century that the idea occurred that there had been an evolution of organic life, and that over long periods of time intelligent minds had developed from animal minds, which in turn had developed from simpler (vegetative) forms of organic life. They had developed from inorganic matter, which gained the capacity to reproduce and mutate.

The theory of evolution began as a philosophical theory, propounded by, among many others, Erasmus Darwin, Charles' grandfather. But with Charles Darwin's *The Origin of Species*, published in 1859, it became a properly scientific hypothesis.

The emphasis now came to be laid on the capacities of various sorts of physical entities. Instead of thinking of minds as separate entities that somehow became embodied in matter, mind could now be thought of as the development of new sorts of capacity in material bodies. Aristotle seemed to be vindicated, in that respect at least.

That said, Aristotle had what would seem for most modern physicists to be an unduly strong teleological view of nature. That is, he thought purpose was built into nature. All things had some sort of purpose (Greek, *telos*), some goal that they were intended to achieve. This goal was, in general, to fulfil their essential natures, to be what they were "meant" to be.

To put it rather strangely, the purpose of a potato was to be a really good potato, to realize as fully as possible all the potentialities that it had as a young potato-seed. The purpose of a tiger was to be a really good tiger, to hunt, kill, and reproduce as really good tigers do. And the purpose of a human being was to be a really good human being, to realize the special potentialities for thinking logically, feeling deeply, and acting creatively that are proper to intelligent minds.

The idea that absolutely everything has a purpose—so that stones, for instance, are trying to get to the center of the earth—has been abandoned in modern physics. Yet some more general notion of purpose in nature still seems plausible. There may be a more general purpose of nature to produce intelligent minds out of insensate matter. That purpose may be realized in many different ways, not all of which are equally effective, though the process will achieve its goal eventually. The goal is already potentially present in the origin of the process, and it may become actual through the independent actions of many finite intelligent minds, as well as through the directing influence of Mind.

For Aristotle, the ideas of potentiality and actuality are really important for understanding nature. A potentiality is a possibility, but not just any possibility. It is a preferred or "proper" possibility, a possibility built into a certain kind of organism as its goal, the reason for its existence. An example of this is the way in which the ideal of a thinking, feeling, acting agent is potential in the human embryo. In cosmic history, humans—intelligent minds—were potential in the animal world, which was itself potential in the plant world, which was potential in inorganic matter, which was potential at the first moment of the Big Bang.

If you look at things this way, the history of the universe is the story of the gradual unfolding of its potentialities, which have been there since the beginning of time. It is only with the origin of intelligent minds that the universe begins to understand, value, and direct its own course. In human communities, the world comes to know, understand, and evaluate itself, to direct its future to a limited extent, and to feel and come to consciousness of its own nature.

If this process continues along the same lines, one can envisage a final state of complete understanding, supreme value, and full control, as an end-point of the process. That would certainly be a state of intrinsic value—that is, a state that is worth existing just for its own sake. Such a state, attained as a result of many stages of development, would be a worthwhile purpose for the existence of a universe. So, with some qualifications, would be the process that leads to it.

It is, of course, far from obvious that such an unfolding process will continue. It is a matter of faith, of trust in the ultimate goodness of being. But even if the process is thought to end with something like human life, the emergence of value, feeling, and purpose was always potential in the material universe. Not only was it possible; it seems to be a possibility built into the universe as its intended worthwhile goal. It would, therefore, be a completely inadequate view to say that the properties of the universe at the moment of the Big Bang were only those that were actual at that time—namely, virtually infinite energy in an unorganized and unstable state. The universe had inherent in it from the first the idea of a worthwhile goal, which was the positive fulfilment of its potentiality.

If this is the case, at the beginning of this universe there existed something that laid down, at least in a general way, if not in every detail, the possible future or futures of the universe. The basic rules would not only have to lay down how fundamental particles like photons and electrons would form and behave. They would also have to lay down that they could, or perhaps that they would have to, develop into relatively stable forms—atoms and molecules. These would develop into cells, nervous systems, and brains. And they would generate emergent properties like knowing, feeling, and willing. There seems to be a vector, a direction of change, governing the development of the universe towards a goal.

The trouble with mental emergent properties is that they are totally unlike purely physical properties like spin, mass, and electro-magnetic charge. We could say that they will be actualized when physical properties reach a certain stage of organized complexity, and that they will depend in detail on the nature of such complex structures. But it is not sensible to say that they are totally unexpected properties that suddenly appear for no reason at all.

Natural science would come to an end if things appeared in the universe without any reason. That would put an end to scientific explanation. There must be laws stating that when physical particles have developed to a specific organized state, new, mental, properties will appear.

The most reasonable thing to say, in my view, is that the mental properties are properties of the physical things, which only appear when the physical things have developed a complex structure. Mental properties are not totally unpredictable surprises. They are properties of objective things that unfold after a long process of development. They are present in various degrees in the animal, and perhaps in the plant world. They express a staged unfolding of the latent potencies of the material world. The feeling that they are in some sense purposive or goal-directed is almost overwhelming.

4. EMERGENCE

There is a pretty wide acceptance among natural scientists that mental properties are emergent properties from the material world. But there is not such a wide acceptance of the idea that they are really entities with distinctive properties of their own. That is, they are features of objective reality that exist in addition to the purely physical properties of velocity, mass, electric and gravitational attraction, and so on. Some people talk about consciousness as though it was nothing more than some sort of interaction between the hundred billion neurons of the human brain.

The model they are thinking of is the model of a society, which is solely made up of lots of individual people, and yet is able to behave and act as a society, a sort of "social individual" that is somehow more than just the sum of its individual parts.

However, nobody thinks that a society really is a conscious individual that has experiences and makes decisions of its own. Sometimes people speak like that, saying things like "The United Kingdom has decided . . . ." But nobody thinks that, in addition to the prime minister, the Parliament, and millions of ordinary citizens, there is a ghostly figure looking over the Houses of Parliament, or perhaps Buckingham Palace, making a decision of her own.

In this case, "United Kingdom" is shorthand for a complex sentence that people cannot be bothered to say, like, "By a complicated process, many adults elected as MPs, who mostly belonged to a political party, and the party that had most MPs chose a prime minister, who met with a cabinet, who had a discussion, which by a majority vote decided that . . . ." It is just not true that the United Kingdom as an entity, nor even all its citizens as individuals, agreed with the decision that was made. But they just had to live with it.

Politically speaking, it is very important to remember that the decisions of a society are made by such a complex process, and that there is no such thing as a universally agreed "will of the people," some sort of super-conscious mind making its own decisions.

When we are thinking about people with minds and bodies, however, the process of thinking and decision-making does not happen like this. Our bodily cells do not vote, our neurons do not debate, and there is no prime minister neuron who comes to a decision after hearing (or, more probably, ignoring, all the arguments). Physically speaking, there are no votes and no debate and no decisions at all. There are just electrical impulses whizzing about the neural network, causing bodies to behave in physically measurable ways.

The brain probably is, as is often said by neuroscientists, made up of various competing sub-systems, which may conflict with or cooperate with each other. But those "competitions" operate on purely mechanical principles. To put it bluntly, the most powerful electrical set of impulses always wins (or always would win if it was not redirected by an act of will), not because it has the best arguments, but because it has the greatest combination of physical forces.

Mental events, like thoughts, feelings, and intentions, are completely different in kind from physical events like gravitational or electro-magnetic interactions. The thought of a future event, for example, occurs at a specific time, and it does exist at that time. But it refers to an event that, at that time, does not exist at all. That is part of its meaning, part of what it is to be a thought, and not just an actual event. The thought is actual, but it is the thought of a possibility, it is a representation.

Thoughts essentially have meaning; they are *about* things that may or may not exist. Physical events are not *about* anything; they just are what they are. This property of being "about," or representing, some object, process, or action, is an internal property of many mental events. Physical events simply do not have such a property.

Feelings, too, have properties not shared by physical events. They give knowledge of "what it is like" to exist as they do, and of whether it is good or bad, pleasant or unpleasant, to be like that.

Thoughts and feeling evoke responses. They call for decisions to be made. They introduce a totally new form of causality into the world. That causality is future-related. It looks to a possible future, evaluates it, and initiates action in order to realize it. Purely physical causes do not refer to the future and are not guided by thoughts of a desirable or undesirable future. They just operate in accordance with pre-set laws, with no concern for the outcome.

Mental events, then, are new entities with new properties, and they operate according to new causal factors. Their emergence from matter is not just a case of matter, with its own properties, interacting in very complex and integrated ways. What emerges are *new kinds* of entity, property, and causal power. In the human case, these new factors could not exist without highly integrated physical systems. Yet they are different in kind.

A fourteen billion-year-long evolutionary development of complex integrated physical systems has given rise to the existence of intelligent minds that can experience and help to create states of intrinsic value. This might well suggest that the laws and fundamental forces of nature are as they are precisely because they will lead to such an outcome.

5. VALUE

That would be a very satisfactory explanation for the existence of the universe. If you say that something is just worth existing for its own sake (like a great piece of art or a state of great happiness), you have answered the question, "Why does it exist?" To say that something is worthwhile for its own sake is a question-stopping explanation, probably the only question-stopping explanation that really works. "I like it" stops anybody asking the question "why?" But "This is something that every rational agent has a good reason to like" is even better.

The notion of value is not one that exists in a purely physical reality. Some people think that values are purely subjective. They are just a matter of what a person prefers. Nobody's preferences are better than anyone else's. Some people like cornflakes. Others prefer oats. Neither is more valuable than the other. Value is not an "objective property," it is just a subjective reaction, which varies from one person to another.

There is a small element of truth in this. If there were no minds that could value things, then there would be no values. There was a philosopher (G. E. Moore) who said that a beautiful universe would be more valuable than an ugly universe, even if there were no minds to appreciate the difference between them. I cannot make any sense of this. It seems to me that a completely unobserved universe would have no actual value. A thing has actual value only if it is worth choosing by a conscious being—which implies that there are conscious beings around capable of evaluation and choice, that have knowledge, feeling, and will.

A state can have *hypothetical* value—that is to say, it could be worthy of choice by a conscious being, if any such being existed. But for a value to be *actual*, there must be some conscious beings who would, or should, choose it, just because it is satisfying. That might sound very subjective. But the catch lies in the phrase "worth choosing." Some states are worth choosing, even if no one chooses them. "Being worthy of choice" is an objective, even though hypothetical, property. It exists whether or not minds exist. Yet it is an actual, as opposed to a hypothetical, property only if there are minds around who could and should choose it.

An actual value is thus a blend of objective and subjective. There is some objective property of a state that needs subjective (i.e., mental) appreciation to become actual. Moore's beautiful universe needs some mind who can observe its beauty before it become an actual value. But when there is such a mind, beauty becomes a commanding value, something that demands the attention and appreciation of any intelligent mind.

Some doubt, or say they doubt, that there are any "objective" values, states that are worth realizing for their own sakes. People aim at all sorts of different things, and there is no point in comparing them as better or worse. I have two things to say about this. First, people do aim at many different things. That is part of human diversity and creativity, and it is a good thing. Yet there are some basic things that *all* rational minds aim at. These are objective values. Objective values, which all rational and feeling beings have a good reason to choose, are such things as: health, survival, pleasure, knowledge, power, and friendship. All rational beings desire a healthy life with enough knowledge and power to achieve pleasant experiences, and enough friends to help attain them.

Second, some human choices are simply corrupted and perverted. We can identify what they are, and then we should discount them as irrational and without enduring value. Unfortunately, there are many irrational beings around, who fail to obtain objective values even when they can. The world is full of unhealthy, short-lived people who are ignorant, weak, and friendless, even though they are capable of living a normal healthy life.

It is reasonable to say that there are objective values. If there is a cosmic Mind, they will be actual values, known by that Mind. They will be hypothetical values for intelligent minds that can later come to know them, as demanding an active response that can make such values actual in new and uniquely creative ways.

6. THE SELF-REALIZING UNIVERSE

This is an emergent world, but it is hard to see it as an accident, blind and pitiless. It is also hard to see it as completely directed by an all-powerful being who always cares for the good of all things (a conscious all-powerful and all-directing God). There are too many conflicts and failures and dead ends for that to be plausible. The process of emergence is multiple, creative, and explorative, ultimately moving towards value and goodness. This appears to be a largely self-realizing cosmos.

At or even before the beginning of the universe a future state of intrinsic value is envisaged, and a process of development towards it from unconscious and relatively unorganized matter is initiated. In other words, there is already meaning, value, and purpose at the beginning of the universe. It is not the value and purpose of anything within the universe itself. It is the envisaged value and developing purpose of a reality beyond our spacetime. That reality is basically mind-like, aiming to bring into existence communities of many other partly self-developing minds that can create and realize new sorts of worthwhile values that would not otherwise exist.

Aristotle thought that the universe (of which the earth was the center) culminated in the existence of aristocratic Greeks. Some Christians have thought that the universe was about to culminate, about four hundred years later, in the existence of a Galilean prophet. Hegel seems to have thought (though this may be a willful misunderstanding) that the universe achieved its goal with him. We know that all were mistaken. It may seem to some of us that the universe actually culminates with us. But it may dawn on us that this is an unduly arrogant thought.

It is more reasonable to postulate that there is a primal reality that generates the simplest possible existent form of being (the Big Bang), and sets it on course to develop a communion of cooperating minds that can at last participate consciously and creatively in the supreme value that has all along been drawing it to itself, what Dante called "the love that moves the sun and other stars."

That culmination may lie beyond the history of the material universe, destined as the universe is to decay and cease to be. Our physical universe would not then be the only or the ultimate reality. Beyond it would lie the Mind that conceived it, that set it on its evolutionary course, and that envisaged from the first the ideal goal towards which it moves. Both in its ultimate origin and in its final consummation, the physical universe points beyond itself to a cosmic Mind that is its origin, basis, and destiny.

On this view, the primal reality of Mind has at least three main aspects: (i) the abyss of potency, (ii) the impetus to realize its potencies in many emergent forms, and (iii) the ideal towards which the cosmos moves. The movement itself is one of real multiple creativity and emergent change towards a goal of supreme value.

If this is true, it might be appropriate to respond to the cosmos with a resolute commitment to value-creation, with patient endurance of present struggles when things are difficult and dangerous, and with hope for future fulfilment. One will not see the world of which one is part as pitilessly and pointlessly indifferent, but as oriented to goodness, though through sacrifice and struggle. And perhaps there is—many people say that there is—a "sense of the presence of a personal power or powers making for goodness."

7. THE UNFOLDING OF MIND

The early Greco-Roman philosopher Plotinus suggested that the supreme supra-cosmic reality, which he called the One, by its nature overflows by creating many different forms of goodness. Goodness, he proposed, is self-diffusive. The One diffuses all possible forms of goodness, down to the very minimum degree of goodness, which is mixed with many elements of chance, disorder, and imperfection. Every possible form of goodness must be manifested, unless it is outweighed by its imperfections, including the imperfection of suffering (in itself a sign of some malfunction in the body).

Natural and moral evils, he thought, are basically privations of goodness; they are the lack of something good, as blindness is the lack of sight, or bodily pain is a sign of some bodily malfunction. In worlds that express the lower degrees of goodness, there will be many such privations of goodness. It may seem that there could be possible worlds that are wholly evil. This, however, is not the case. If evil is a privation, or a sign of the malfunction of something that is basically good, there cannot be a world of *pure* privation. That is not a possible world. It is nothing.

Thus, the lowest possible world will manifest the lowest forms of goodness, together with many privations and imperfections. But it will still manifest many forms of goodness that would not otherwise exist at all. It may even be possible that such privations as exist in it can be remedied, and that the goodness in that world can in some higher form be reinforced, fully expressed, and cleared of all imperfection. Plotinus spoke of a "return to the One" as the destiny even of things existing at the lowest level of being.

Evil can thus exist in a cosmic order that is good overall on three main conditions. (1) It must be necessary, or unavoidable. (2) It must be as little in degree as possible. And (3) it must be hugely outweighed by a subsequent good, which could only originate in a world containing these imperfections, a good that can be experienced by all who have suffered evil.

Tradition is right in saying that there are two basic kinds of evil that can meet such conditions. One is the evils that must exist in a world that permits the development of intelligent minds by means of general and intelligible laws, open alternatives, the attraction—real but resistable—of ideal goals, and the exercise of virtue. This is usually called "natural evil." The other is the evils that necessarily follow from egocentric, impulsive, and short-sighted choices made by sentient beings that impede such development. This is "moral evil."

Plotinus had no idea of evolution, so he saw world-stages with all possible degrees of goodness descending from the perfect. A modern evolutionary view would instead see the cosmos as ascending in complexity towards the development of many self-realizing intelligent minds.

This might change our idea of Mind, the source of all things, as not a wholly perfect being from which all lower forms of goodness descend. It might instead be the ground of all possibility, striving to realize its own inner potencies ultimately through its creative relationship with an emergent community of intelligent minds, united in creativity and compassion.

In such a world, we humans would be parts of a process of forging beauty, understanding, creativity, cooperation, and compassion out of chaos, destruction, and conflict. We can align ourselves with the struggle for good, endure trials with patience, and hope for the victory of the good. In the Christian tradition, St. Paul spoke of the virtues of faith, hope, and love. Put in less specifically Christian terms, we could say that faith is trust in the presence of a higher power for good; hope is the anticipation of its ultimate success; and love is practical action for the welfare of all beings, which can be strengthened by being open to and mediating something of the power for good which lies at the basis of our physical cosmos.

It might be misleading to say of Mind that it is an absolutely omniscient and omnipotent God, or even to say that "God is love," if this gives rise to the idea that God would never cause harm to intelligent minds, a belief that flies in the face of human experience of disaster and grief. However, it could be possible to say that "God is on the side of love," and even that "God is the power of love that can work within us, and that will be ultimately fulfilled in and through us." In that sense, we could say that God is the suffering, demanding, empowering, and ultimately victorious power of love. If we prefer not to use the term "God," we could still speak of a Mind or Spirit, which unfolds its own nature in the universe in and through the generation of communities of creative minds that are meant to relate to each other in wisdom and love.

ABSTRACT OF THE ARGUMENT
IN PARTS ONE AND TWO

At this point it may be helpful to distil the essence of my argument so far.

Part One: Mind

- All knowledge begins with experience—perceptions, sensations, feelings, thoughts, intentions, memories.

- Sensory spaces are private and unique. This is clearest in dreams, in unspoken thoughts, and in indescribable feelings.

- Feelings exist; they add something to the kinds of things that exist. Even to "identify" them with brain-events, something (electrical events in the brain) is being identified with *something else* (a feeling of depression), and a constant conjunction is being asserted.

- Such conjunctions may exist, but they are logically contingent.

- There is more to the world than collections of physical objects. There is "inner life."

- When I understand something, I observe, classify, imagine, theorize. These are creative exercises of skill, of critical enquiry. When I paint a picture, I create order and pattern. I change the world. When I interact with others, I may choose to be helpful or egoistical. I have a moral choice. We are enquiring, creative, and moral agents. In and through us the cosmos itself is value-creating.

- Our experience includes understanding and responding, which means that active classification, interpretation, and freedom of response are all involved in experience. It is not just passive occurrence of data; it is data as interpreted and processed, in an active stream of experience that is essentially interactive, not purely individual.

- We can envisage a possible final goal of this process in maximal knowledge, understanding, experienced value, and creative relationship. But such a goal must be won by struggle and endeavor.

Part Two: Cosmos

- The history of the cosmos is a story of the emergence of many experiencing and creative agents from a primal state of undifferentiated energy (the "Big Bang"). There is an emergent trajectory towards greater self-understanding and self-direction of the cosmic order, towards the free creation and consciousness of many worthwhile states and processes, an unfolding of potencies that are presumably present at the origin of the cosmos.

- From the beginning, potentialities exist that are oriented towards the actualization of communities of feeling and creative agents. As parts of this unfolding process, humans form, realize, and enjoy values that become purposes for us. We cooperate with the value-creating tendencies of the cosmos, realizing in multiple unique ways the possibilities of value it contains.

- The existence of such a value-actualizing cosmos suggests a reality that possesses the potentiality of consciously created and experienced values, generates a cosmic impetus towards their realization, and suggests the possibility of a final transformation and completion of their history. The process appears to unfold by necessity throughout many possible grades of being, emergently evolving from a state of unconscious, undifferentiated being without organization or integration, complexity, or intelligible law, without inherent purpose or value, the minimal limit of possible being, to communities of conscious purposive creators and appreciators of value.

- This emergence, or evolution, appears to be directed towards the realization of values, yet the process involves competition, destruction, decay, and death, as well as cooperation, creation, organization, and life. The inexorable decay of the overall energy of the universe (the law of cosmic entropy) makes possible local systems of highly integrated complexity (the emergence of intelligent feeling and purpose). This is neither a wholly blind and accidental process nor one directed in every detail to good outcomes by an all-determining God. It is a process characterized by risk and failure yet tending towards good. It is not *wholly* caused by a divine will, which consciously intends always to do what is good. The cosmic process realizes possibilities that emanate by necessity, letting them form themselves, guided by a general attraction of the Good, in a creative/conflictual/cooperative process leading to the formation of sentient agents who can consciously co-operate with the power for goodness. The ultimate reality, in this view, is Mind, the abyss of possibility, the power making for goodness, and the completion of the realized goodness of the cosmos.

Part Three

VIRTUE

In Part One, I expounded the nature of human existence as a developing unity of creative and intelligent minds, which, if they act together in positive ways, will realize distinctive forms of intrinsic value.

In Part Two, I related human existence to its place in the cosmos, which itself can be seen as the progressive unfolding of intrinsic values out of the formless abyss of potential being.

In Part Three, I will explore the implications of these views for human action in the world.

1. TRUTH

The most obvious feature of the descriptions of humanity and the cosmos that I have given is the centrality of the notions of purpose and value. These notions have little or no place in the natural sciences, at least as presently conceived. Yet the natural sciences often find great value in the beauty and organized complexity of the natural world, and they often have the purpose of understanding the world and using that knowledge to pursue the further purpose of improving the quality of human lives.

In that way, natural scientists are themselves often outstanding practitioners of purposive action aiming at the production of values. This is one of the great virtues of human life. It is what Aristotle called an intellectual virtue, and it does not have to rely on any sort of belief in a cosmic Mind, whether this is called God or nor. Or at least, that is how it seems. In fact, modern scientists are sometimes strongly opposed to anything like religion. There is no God, they think, who heals people dying from cancer, or who makes sure that believers escape from natural disasters.

Einstein thought that the Hebrew Bible was a collection of legends and absurd regulations; though Jewish, he was not religious. But he did not mock the idea that there was a vast but rather inscrutable intelligence underlying the mathematically beautiful and intelligible laws of nature. He also had a strong belief, stronger than the evidence suggested, that "God did not play dice with the universe"; which means, I think, that there is an intelligible reason for everything that happens.

The practice of good science presupposes other things, too. It presupposes that the universe can be understood by human minds, that the search for truth is of vital importance, that trust in the honesty of one's colleagues is essential, and that it is important to support one's beliefs by evidence, impartially obtained and subjected to sustained criticism.

These are strong beliefs. They can sustain a lifetime of intense labor, and they face temptations to put the desire for fame before patient investigation, or to massage the evidence to support what is in fact a prejudice. Concern for truth, honesty, and trust, for human welfare, and loving attention to some aspect of the natural world—all these are important in the pursuit of natural science.

These things can be pursued for their own sake, without any conscious commitment to a largescale view of what reality is ultimately like. But suppose you do take the view that reality is ultimately mind-like in nature, rather than a set of unconscious, non-purposive exchanges of brute energies. Then understanding and rationality will be fundamental features of reality. Whatever laws of nature there are, they will be intelligible. Everything will happen for a reason, which might only be discernible by those who see the history of the universe as a whole. There will be a beauty in the structure of being, since it is the contemplated object of a Mind that is older and greater than any human mind.

If intelligent minds emerge within this universe, they too will have value and purpose. One of their purposes will be to increase understanding of the world, to explore and investigate, to seek truth and to avoid ignorance and deception. One of their greatest values will be knowledge and understanding, and it will be wrong to do anything that impedes the growth of knowledge—even if what impedes it is some allegedly revealed doctrine in some ancient text.

That is probably why some scientists distrust religion—because they think religion is often based on weakly evidenced historical claims, or claims certainty for things that are highly disputable, or proclaims beliefs that it does not allow to be criticized. To be brutally direct, if some form of religion does that, it ought to be renounced for the sake of truth.

What is happening in that case is that commitment to some alleged untestable revelation is being replaced by commitment to the supreme value of truth and understanding. But it must be seen that such a commitment is also untestable. How could we test the belief that truth is supremely worthwhile? It is a matter of faith, faith in truth as an intrinsic value and a worthy human purpose.

Faith in truth does not need to be based on faith that there is a cosmic Mind; it stands on its own. But there are four main elements that idealism adds to such a heroic and indeed admirable stance. First, faith that there is a cosmic Mind, when rightly understood, entails faith in truth as a value and purpose that is not just invented by humans, but that is written into the very fabric of the universe. If the ultimate reality is a cosmic Mind, then in responding to an objective purpose, you are responding to a Mind that has that purpose, and that invites you to cooperate in realizing the purpose.

This introduces an element of personal loyalty and trust into your picture of the world. In aiming at truth and understanding, you are not just responding to some impersonal value, which may be unaware of your response and unchanged by whatever you do.

You are responding to a personal demand, or better, to a personal invitation, to share in realizing some value. And what you do will produce a change in the cosmic Mind itself, as it apprehends and reacts in a personal way to your decision. Morality becomes not just obedience to an impersonal and commanding duty, good though that may be. It becomes part of a cooperating relationship with a personal reality whose values and purposes are shared with your own.

Second, if this is the case, the cosmic Mind may actually empower your efforts to cooperate, acting in and through you to strengthen your will and deepen your understanding. Moral action will then not just be heroic reliance on your own powers. It may become a cooperation with a power greater than your own, which is able to act through you. In various religions this is known as "grace," "other-power," or "the action of the true self." In non-religious contexts, it may still be felt, even in the natural sciences, as inspiration or intuition, which suddenly or unexpectedly brings deeper understanding, that does not seem to be the result of any purely rational process.

Third, those who believe that moral ideals are rooted in a cosmic Mind that seeks to bring order and creative beauty out of chaotic and self-destructive powers are likely to believe that goodness will find fulfilment. Understanding will increase, and ignorance and deceit will be progressively overcome, so that the purpose of being will eventually be realized. Whether that is within this universe or beyond it, in other realms of being, there will be a full realization of value and an elimination of evil and suffering. Such a hope for the victory of goodness seems realistic only when Mind is seen as the ultimate reality. Such a hope tends to strengthen moral commitment, since it posits that moral struggle will not be in vain, and that the cosmos will not end with a whimper of failed desires and shattered ideals. Of course, materialist moralists may be content with lesser and more temporary gains, or may even do what is right without any hope that good will come. I think it is clear, however, that an idealist belief will engender a sure hope that is founded on a rationally intelligible account of human moral striving.

Fourth, if it is believed that all finite experiences will be apprehended by the cosmic Mind, and will be held there without forgetfulness; if that Mind has the power to bring good out of the evils that many finite minds have had to endure; and if there will eventually be a full realization of good and the elimination of evil; then it is reasonable to hope that all the finite minds that have ever existed will have the possibility of consciously sharing in that realization.

This is a matter of faith, of trust in the goodness of being. But such faith, though it can never be certain, is strongly coherent with acceptance of the primacy of Mind, its values, and its purposes. And, for many, it is supported by their experience of a loving presence that is other and more than human, and whose purpose is powerful and good.

What I have tried to do is to show that there are fundamental values that demand human allegiance. They evoke virtues that are distinctive to human beings, whatever theoretical beliefs about reality humans have. One of these virtues is the intellectual virtue of truth and understanding. Natural scientists often provide exemplary examples of this virtue, but they often deny the idealist view that the ultimate basis of reality is Mind.

I suggest that such commitment to the objective force of moral ideals implies that there is more to reality than purely physical entities and interactions. Both the belief that nature is intelligible and comprehensible, and the belief that intellectual understanding is a human excellence of intrinsic value, point to features of reality that are not physical, but are of major importance. They point to a rational structure in nature and a worthwhile purpose that belongs to human existence that are not just based on purely personal and subjective decisions.

There does not have to be any theoretical justification for a belief that truth and understanding are objectively demanding ideals, and it could be disappointing to a scientist to have beliefs that do not fit easily into the official creed of materialism. Yet materialism is also a presupposition that goes well beyond the evidence, and in that sense does not have an independent justification. I have not intended to give a proof of idealism, but to indicate that idealism provides a coherent framework within which both the mathematical beauty of nature and the objective moral purpose of pursuing truth and understanding can find a natural place.

For the moment, my concern is with what acceptance of the primacy of Mind implies for human action. So far, I have argued that it would place the pursuit of truth and understanding as intellectual virtues that are proper to human life. These virtues outline a purpose for humans, and for any intelligent minds, that is of intrinsic value.

2. BEAUTY

As well as the intellectual virtues of pursuing truth and understanding, there are aesthetic virtues that it is proper for intelligent minds to pursue. These are the virtues of creating and appreciating beauty, in face of the forces of decay and indifference that are present in our universe.

The creation of beauty covers such simple things as cultivating a garden or fashioning a piece of furniture, as well as the production of great paintings, music, and literature. The appreciation of beauty ranges from admiring a landscape to listening to a Beethoven symphony or being moved by the poetry of Keats.

All these things are of intrinsic value; they are things or activities that are worthwhile just for their own sake. But they take effort to achieve, and so they are virtues or human excellences that realize the distinctive potentialities of human nature. If you ask the question about which things are worthwhile in life, the answer lies largely in *these* things. One important human purpose is their achievement.

If there is a cosmic Mind which wills to realize intrinsic values through the activities of finite intelligent minds, these are some of the important values that the cosmic Mind would will and decree as distinctive human purposes.

As with truth, beauty can be pursued without any reference to such a thing as a cosmic Mind. A form of humanism that is totally agnostic about metaphysical questions concerning the nature of ultimate reality will rightly stress the importance of creating and appreciating beauty. That is part of what it is to promote human well-being, and so it is a true *human*ism, a concern with human good.

But there are serious questions about whether this concern is just a rather human-centered and subjective preference for the welfare of one biological species on this planet. Beauty might be a real feature of objective reality, which demands or invites the attention of any form of intelligent mind. The creation of beautiful things may be the realization of the distinctive capacities of any intelligent mind, capacities that are not just accidental products of a blind evolution but are emergent from and proper to the nature of the cosmos itself.

When we attend to and love beauty, we are not just following some transient subjective preference. We are being taken out of our own fluctuating and self-centered desires by focusing our attention on something that is worthwhile in itself. The love of beauty is the love of something other than ourselves and our preferences. It is losing the sense of self in the contemplation of what is good just for its own sake. We do not think beauty is good because we prefer it. We ought to prefer it because it is good.

If we have such a sense of beauty, we may see many things in the world as beautiful. Then we are seeing something more than physical properties. We are seeing value as something present in the world. Perhaps this is not so much humanism—concern with human welfare—as it is the recognition of something other than human, other than physical, which is expressed in the physical and perceived by the human, but is other than both.

In those moments of perception, the world becomes transparent to value. Human attempts to create beauty become attempts to bring to light what is already there. Then we may think that the physical universe is not valueless and indifferent to intelligent life. For the universe has brought intelligent life into being, and has forged beauty out of the life of the stars. Even in the seemingly endless emptiness of interstellar space, there is strange and awe-inspiring beauty. It is not absurd to see this as the work of intelligent Mind, which brings beauty out of insensate matter, and contemplates that beauty long before there are human minds to share that contemplation.

Just as beauty may be an objective value of being, so the creation of beauty may be an objective purpose of being. Creators of great works of art often speak of themselves, at their best, as instruments of some creative power that is felt to work through them. Beethoven, for example, wrote, "What we conquer for ourselves through art is from God, divine inspiration . . . , every genuine creation of art is independent; mightier than the artist himself." Many creative artists have had this sense that inspiration, "the Muse," sometimes descends upon them, so that they become channels as much as originators of beauty.

Not many of us have such gifts. For that is what they are, gifts of nature, not self-originated, though ours is the responsibility for using them. Of course, this is not a proof of God, especially not of the bearded humanoid person who has been depicted as God in much of Western art. It is an intimation that there are creative powers in nature that originate in nature itself, and that intelligent minds can mediate, with various degrees of effectiveness.

Some people say that if the cosmos has purposes and values, we have no idea of what they are. The Nobel prize winning physicist Stephen Weinberg made a comment to this effect that has become famous: "the more the universe seems comprehensible, the more it also seems pointless." Yet Weinberg also said, "It is possible that there is only one logically isolated theory . . . that is consistent with the existence of intelligent beings." Perhaps the laws of the universe have to be what they are to produce intelligent beings like us. We are beings that can create and love beauty. The love of beauty is a great intrinsic good. Therefore, the universe is not pointless. It *has* to be the way it is to produce these great intrinsic goods. That is its point and purpose. We can know and understand that. It is our responsibility to participate in the realization of that purpose, which is not just our subjective choice, but which has been potential in the cosmos from its beginning.

If idealism is true, if there is a cosmic Mind, then one purpose of human life is to create and to love beauty, in its many different forms. For an idealist, beauty will be an objective property of being that commands our attention. The universe will be a source of creative powers that enable us to create new forms of beauty. The purpose of the cosmos itself will be to become the unobstructed expression and vehicle, the physical image, of beauty. There is reason to hope that this purpose will be fully realized, and that many, perhaps all, intelligent minds will be able to participate in the creation and contemplation of perfected beauty, when that realization is complete.

It is important to stress that there are many forms and degrees of beauty. Very few people can create great art, music, or literature. Most of us, however, can appreciate what they do. And we can all do something to create and love beauty. Keeping a room or garden clean is the creation of beauty. Attending to and savoring the tastes, sounds, and sights that we experience in everyday life is the love of beauty.

All that is required of us is to do the best of which we are capable. The tragedy is that there are those who do not love beauty, who will destroy the environment for the sake of commercial gain, or who will limit or destroy the efforts of others to be creative. Truth and beauty are the values and purposes of being, but there are those who will lie, destroy, and oppress to gain power over others, and to obtain fame or pleasure for themselves.

These things, too, are possibilities of being. Because of that, we need to recognize the importance of moral virtues, especially the virtues of cooperation and compassion, which are an essential aspect of human existence.

3. LOVE

Human beings are not isolated minds who are primarily concerned with their own fulfilment. Humans are members of communities, and fulfilment cannot be achieved in isolation from others. If we want to create music, we need others to play it, and others to teach us how to write it. If we want to make new scientific discoveries, we depend on others to teach us the practices of good science, and to help us in our research. If we are concerned to find lasting happiness, one of the greatest forms of happiness is loving relationship to other persons.

Many of us know that being in love with another person, delighting in their company, sharing experiences with them, and caring for them when they are in need, can make our lives feel more meaningful and bring us great happiness. "Being in love" is perhaps a rather rare experience, that comes to us unexpectedly and often does not endure with its initial intensity. Loving another person, however, is something that takes a lot of hard work, as we learn to live with their foibles and come to terms with our differences of viewpoint. It is, however, deeper and richer than a short and intense period of infatuation with another. It involves caring for their welfare for better and for worse, and building up a relationship of trust and loyalty that can endure many hardships and disappointments.

Genuine friendship shows that happiness is not to be found in self-gratification, or in having a relationship because of the good things it brings to the one who loves. Genuine friendship is centered on the other, and it brings the greatest happiness only when it is the happiness of the other that is sought. The paradox of love is that only if you care for the happiness of another for their sake will you discover the greatest happiness for yourself. As many great sages of the past have said, only if you renounce yourself will you find yourself.

This is a difficult saying, for it may lead to a servile subjugation of oneself, and the loss of any sense of pride in one's own achievements and abilities. Some feminists have taken particular objection to the thought that one should be content with serving others, when women throughout the ages have been forced into serving men, whether they like it or not.

What this shows is that the virtue of love (care for the other's welfare) should not be thought of in isolation from other human virtues, including the intellectual and aesthetic virtues. You should aim at realizing the intellectual and aesthetic potentialities of your own nature. You must seek knowledge and understanding, creativity and love of beauty, and you must of course seek these things for yourself. Personal fulfilment is a moral demand.

Relationships with others should therefore be aimed at helping such personal fulfilment. Any relationship that completely subordinates one's own fulfilment to that of another, especially if it is not freely chosen, is inadequate, even immoral. Friendships should be mutually fulfilling. If they are, care for the other's welfare will be present already in the acknowledgement of the other's full humanity. Thus, the virtues of self-realization and of genuine altruism must be held in balance. You cannot realize your own potential if you do not care for others. And you cannot care properly for others if you yourself have not realized at least to some extent your own intellectual and artistic gifts. After all, the more you have to give the better.

Human situations are widely varied, and it is impossible to provide one easy formula to cover all of them. Sometimes real personal sacrifice will be needed when others are in desperate need. Sometimes pursuing great artistic projects will impair one's ability to help others. One needs to attend very carefully to particular difficult situations, and refrain from being too quick to judge or condemn, or from thinking that there is an easy solution to real moral dilemmas.

Nevertheless, the general point stands, that cooperation and empathy with others, the virtues of love, are moral virtues that are necessary to counteract the tendencies to egoism and unconcern for others that are prevalent in human life.

These virtues are found in many people who have no thoughts about either materialism or idealism, and who may regard such speculations as irrelevant to the practical obligation to build fulfilling friendships and care for those in need.

4. IDEALISM AND VIRTUES

What, then, is the relevance of philosophical idealism to these virtues? I absolutely agree that practical conduct and a commitment to moral action, to virtue, is the most important aspect of human life. I absolutely prioritize moral action over theoretical speculation.

However, there are times when some people begin to ask themselves, "Why should I care for others? I can see why I should care for my family and friends, but why should I care about human beings in general? Should I care for animals? Does it really matter if I ignore the needs of people I have never even met?"

Such questions, if they occur, lead people to ask about the importance of morality. I have heard people say, "That is only a moral issue," as though it is much less important than the need to make a profit. And there are many voices that say that morality is some sort of outmoded evolutionary device for getting people to conform or obey authority. There is a real question about the *basis* of morality.

There are many ways of answering such questions. If you are an idealist, if you think Mind is the basis of reality, you will almost certainly place moral obligations in the cosmic Mind. That Mind contains many truths—many thoughts with content—that just have to be the way they are. Among them are the basic truths of mathematics, maybe many truths about what has to exist if there are to be communities of intelligent minds in the cosmos, and many moral truths.

A truth like, "People should care for those in need" is a thought in the cosmic Mind that lays down the conditions for the creation and maintenance of intrinsic values in the cosmos. It derives from a more general thought, like, "Intelligent minds that are members of cooperating creative communities will realize their potentialities maximally if they care for each other's welfare."

When intelligent minds reflect on how to act, they will eventually see that this proposition is true. It does not depend on any supernatural revelation. But why should they care about it?

Because it is not just a statement; it is a recommendation. It says, "This is how intelligent minds should act, if the purpose of the cosmos is to be realized." And it adds, "I want this purpose to be realized."

Now the question becomes, "Why should I do what the cosmic Mind wants?" This is a real question, which each person must answer for themselves. But it is not the same as the question, "Why should I care about other people?"

I think that there is a purpose for the cosmos; it is the purpose of a being of great beauty, understanding, and power, who may help me to achieve the purpose; it is a good purpose, leading to the existence of great intrinsic values; it will be difficult to achieve, but it can and will be achieved; and I can contribute to and share in that achievement.

If I think all these things, it would be irrational not to act as well as I can on the recommendation of the cosmic Mind. There would be an overwhelmingly sufficient reason for accepting the moral obligation to love both the Mind that decreed these things, the good things of the world that it had brought into being, and the other intelligent minds that could cooperate with me in creating intrinsic values.

All these things can be doubted. There may be no purpose for the cosmos; there may be no cosmic Mind; even if there is a purpose, it may never be achieved; and even if it is, I am most unlikely to share in it. Materialists are likely to think all these things. For them, to believe in a cosmic Mind would be justifying morality by appeal to a fantasy.

Yet if there is a good and powerful (not necessarily all-powerful) cosmic Mind, there is a solid rational justification for a sense of authoritative moral obligation. This does not mean that a sense of moral obligation proves that there is anything like a God (that would be a well-known logical fallacy). But the sense that there is an objective demand, not just invented by us, to do or avoid something, gives reason for thinking that there is a non-physical aspect to the reality we experience. Obligations *really* exist. Full-blown theism might not be true; but materialism can seem unduly restrictive, and moral experience can seem to be of a reality that is non-physical and authoritative over human life. If so, it is *other than* and *greater than* the physical.

Furthermore, reflection on this fact may lead us to extend the range of our moral concern—to enemies, to animals, to the earth itself—as it leads us to a less human-centered and more universal view of existence; to seeing things, not just from our ego-centered point of view, but, as the philosopher Spinoza put it, *sub specie aeternitatis*, in the light of eternity.

As we reflect on the meaning of human existence, it may become clear that the most meaningful life will not be one that is centered on one's own pleasure and happiness, perhaps to the detriment of others. A life of pleasure and personal consumption may come to seem empty and meaningless. What gives meaning to life is being centered on states and processes that are of intrinsic value. Such states are realized by the exercise of the distinctive capacities of human being, the capacity for intellectual thought, for responsive and sensitive feeling, and for purposive action.

Such a life is the life of true virtue, and it leaves as its inheritance a unique contribution, however simple it might seem, to the value of the world. Truth and understanding, beauty and creativity, friendship and love of others—these are the values to which each intelligent mind can make a contribution that could be made by no-one else. They are the values contribution to which makes life meaningful and worthwhile.

That contribution can be made whether one is an idealist or not. However, an idealist faith, that these values are objective purposes of the Mind that is expressed in our cosmos, gives them an *objectivity*, an *authority*, and a *durability*, which can immeasurably strengthen our commitment to them.

Part Four

AFTERLIFE

1. THE LIFE TO COME

IT MAY BE ENOUGH to say that our lives contribute in unique ways to states of intrinsic value, even if those states, like all the states of our physical universe, will inevitably pass into nothingness as our planet, and eventually the whole physical universe, dies. It may be enough to say that truth, beauty, and goodness exist and that the struggles to bring them into being have been laudable.

Yet if everything that exists is an expression of Mind, we can reasonably assume that all good things will be known by that Mind, and will continue to be held in that Mind, even beyond the existence of the physical universe, which is only one of the expressions of its being. Thus, the good that we have done will never pass into nothingness and be forgotten, as though it had never been. It will be written into a life and consciousness "beyond the stars."

But we will also have reason to hope that it is not only in one supra-cosmic Mind that these things will endure. We know that such a Mind has the *power* to generate this universe, the *goodness* to place in it the ideals of truth, beauty, and love, and the *purpose* of bringing the perfection of value out of the ambiguous primordial reality of the physical world. We know that it has desired to create finite intelligent minds with whom it can cooperate in creativity and to whom it can relate in love.

Will it not then finally realize that purpose and enable it to be known and experienced by the minds that it has brought into being? The bodies in which those minds were conceived and in which they lived out their lives inevitably perish and are no more. Yet mind is the primal reality, which does not wholly depend upon matter for its existence.

Finite minds need some world to provide the material content of their experience, to enable them to respond creatively to it, and to work together in loving communion. But that world need not have the qualities of this material universe, which is governed by the law of entropy, bringing inevitable decay and death.

It may have been necessary that an entropic world should exist, and give rise to embodied minds, in order to realize the distinctive forms of goodness that only such a world could produce. But it does not seem necessary that minds are tied to the physical world forever. They could be re-embodied in a different realm of being, a different form of universe, a spiritual world with laws and processes very different from those of our material universe, a world where disease and decay do not exist.

Modern cosmology is familiar with the idea that there could be other universes in existence, of very different forms than our own. That is no longer an absurd or fantastic notion. Of course, what I am proposing requires that we can move between universes. But even the thought that consciousness can in principle be transferred from a carbon-based organic body to some other form (say, a silicon-based computer) is canvassed by some responsible scientists. So, a transfer of consciousness and personality to another form is not precluded by scientific thought. If you have the belief that there is a Mind that can generate many universes and has immense power, the transfer of the mind between a material and a different form of universe becomes a realistic possibility.

The hope of personal idealism is that we will die physically, but we will be re-embodied in a spiritual realm. There we will be able to share in the experience of all the good things that have been preserved in Mind itself, in ways and to the degree that they become available to us in our new form of existence.

Such a hope is especially important, because of the tragedy and suffering of so many millions of humans, and perhaps of other intelligent beings also, in the physical universe. If their lives are to have meaning and purpose, it is virtually necessary that they should have the possibility of completion after their physical deaths.

The life of the world to come will not be a simple transfer of this body to a wonderful paradise. It will be a *re*-embodiment in a form that is appropriate to how people have lived on this planet. What that form will be like and what the conditions of that world will be is very hard to imagine. We can only ask what seems to us appropriate in a world ordered by a supreme Mind to fulfil the values that have so often been only incompletely realized in this physical cosmos.

It is possible that even such a Mind has not the power to eliminate evil altogether, and it is possible that even if there is a life beyond this one, it is so different from anything we can conceive that there is not much we should say about it. Perhaps we should follow some Buddhist views and take the stance that we should neither say that we do *not* exist after death nor that we *do* exist after death. We should simply say that we have "gone beyond." Or perhaps we might say that after our physical deaths we will in some fashion share in the eternity of God, without claiming to be able to describe such a state further.

Nevertheless, I believe that a personal idealism that affirms the reality of a supreme Mind with the power to generate living beings and to place before them the binding ideals of truth, beauty, and goodness, must generate in them the hope that there can truly be a full realization of these ideals. Such a full realization would have to be one in which understanding, beauty, and love would be free of the suffering and frustration of the physical world in which they were first fashioned. It would be one in which these ideals were shared in a communion of being that might not be adequately describable by us, but would at least not be less than the best we can imagine. It is in that spirit that I offer the following reflections.

If there is a world to come, in it there will be those who have lived lives committed to goodness. They will probably need to learn much about the true nature of reality, as all of us have probably had many inadequate ideas about reality. But they will enter, one assumes, a realm of loving communion, where they can continue to grow in relationship with beings of many different sorts, from worlds they have never known, and with the Mind that is the storehouse of all the good things that those worlds have produced. Once entered, that communion will be without the possibility of loss, for it is a sharing in the being of Mind itself.

There are people whose lives have been cut short by death, or who have suffered terribly during life. It would be just for them to have the opportunity to develop talents they had that were never used, or to find new ways to happiness and fulfilment. So, the world to come would offer opportunities for growth and development. It would also continue to offer moral choices, which would lead to either growth or decay. The afterlife, like this life, would contain paths leading to great happiness and paths leading to self-inflicted misery and anguish. There would presumably not be just one state of complete happiness ("heaven") and another state of complete misery ("hell"), into which people would be locked forever. There would be great happiness and there would be great misery, but for many people the paths leading to and from them would be open.

Then there would be people who during their earthly lives had chosen evil, egoism, hatred, and greed. The only way of imagining what it would be like for them is to ask what a perfectly benevolent and just Mind would be likely to decree for them. I think that such a Mind would always be concerned for their welfare, and so would leave open paths to happiness. But evil cannot go unheeded. Culprits must be brought to recognition of the evil they have done, and they must be prepared to do whatever can be done to compensate for it, and to re-orient their mind to goodness.

I imagine that some might remain lost in hatred and resentment. For them, the only possibility would eventually be non-existence. After many efforts have been made to change them, they would cease to be. For others, hopefully for many others, possibly for all, a change of mind would be possible. Then they would join those who walk the path towards the indestructible happiness of conscious sharing in Mind.

These thoughts are not founded on any particular religious revelation. They are attempts to imagine what the realized purpose of Mind could be, and depend upon faith that the human mind is capable of reasoning about such things. The necessary presuppositions are that there is a cosmic Mind, that it is concerned with the realization of value and with the welfare of intelligent minds, and that it has the power to bring about its purposes.

I have myself thrown doubt on the traditional view that there is a God who is absolutely omnipotent (i.e., can do anything), knows the future completely and in detail, and is completely changeless. So, it may well be thought that traditional views of life after death—whether people believe in reincarnation or in resurrection, for instance—may have to go as well. I accept that what I have said is about a form of existence that I have not and cannot have experienced for myself. It is based on my belief that since the ultimate reality is Mind, it is possible that human minds could survive the death of their physical bodies. It is also firmly founded on a belief about what a supreme Mind that is good and powerful is likely to do, given the nature of this world. It is hope, and not knowledge. But it is a hope based on a reasoned belief in the priority of mind.

CONCLUSION

IF I AM WRONG about my speculations about life after death in Part Four, and if I have not quite got things right about the evolutionary history of the universe in Part Two, I remain convinced that my arguments in Parts One and Three—on human consciousness as the primary ground of human knowledge and on the key insights into morality that this provides—are valid and important. I do not think a philosopher can hope for more than that, even though many philosophers, and even more theologians, tend to claim much more for their arguments.

I think that personal idealism is the most coherent and plausible general theory about the nature of reality and of human existence. I have presented the case for this without any reference to the doctrines of any religion. Many religions speak of a nonmaterial reality and of ways to relate to it. Some call that reality "God," but it is also thought of as "Pure Mind," "the *Dharmakaya*," "*Brahman*," or "the *Tao*."

These ways are by no means all the same. What is common to many of them is the thought that human lives are estranged from knowledge of this spiritual reality. Various religions offer ways of overcoming that estrangement, whether by personal devotion (love of Jesus or Krishna), moral commitment (to justice and mercy), or a sense of union (*fana*, beatitude, or Buddha realization).

I have written about these things elsewhere, and all I would say in the context of this book is that many of these ways can be seen as complementary—different but effective—means to an apprehension of Mind as I have described it.

There are experts and leading practitioners in science, music, and morality, and if what I have said about Mind is true, there will almost certainly also be people who have a deeper and more adequate apprehension of Mind. They include such people as Jesus, Mohammed, Sankara, Gautama Buddha, and Guru Nanak, as well as many other lesser-known figures.

I would think that their views will be culturally and historically influenced. If so, they will be incorporated into wider beliefs held at their time and in their culture, which will place some constraints on the way they describe their experiences and recommendations. Such constraints may need to be reinterpreted in the light of new knowledge that has accrued in subsequent history.

Nevertheless, the testimony to experience of a higher spiritual reality that they provide is so impressive that it raises the probability that such a reality exists, and can have a positive impact on human lives. Personal idealists do not have to belong to any particular religion, but many who do may be able to use insights derived from this philosophy to interpret their own traditions.

Is the universe in which we exist a reality of blind, pitiless indifference? Or is it the expression of conscious Mind, with a purpose of fulfilment for all beings? This is a key question for all human beings.

What has provided new resources for thinking about this question is the development of an evolutionary view of the universe, an increased sense that humans are free and responsible agents of their own destiny, an expanded awareness of the extent of suffering and destruction in our universe, and an appreciation of how difficult it is to reconcile the facts of consciousness with the materialistic presuppositions of many modern natural scientists.

The form of personal idealism I have presented tries to use these resources to provide a coherent and plausible view of the place of human beings in our vast universe. The view is one that provides a firm place for faith in an optimistic future for humanity, and a firm foundation for believing in the authority and importance of morality. It finds the ultimate meaning of life in a creative relation to a Mind, which has the ultimate purpose of enabling all beings to share in its own life. For that reason, it is not just some abstract theory, only of interest to expert philosophers. It is of vital interest to every thinking person to decide whether it is true.

APPENDIX

Some additional notes for those interested
in further reading or exploration

PART ONE: MIND

PROFESSOR RICHARD DAWKINS IS an Oxford colleague whose
work I value enormously, though I disagree almost completely
with his philosophical views, as should be obvious. My shortest
and sharpest response to some of his views can be found in: *Why
There Almost Certainly Is a God* (Oxford: Lion Hudson, 2008).

I have given two accounts of personal idealism in: *More Than
Matter* (Oxford: Lion Hudson, 2010), largely responding to the influential work of my one-time philosophy tutor Gilbert Ryle, and
in *The Christian God* (Cambridge: Cambridge University Press,
2017), which gives a more fully theistic interpretation.

Some form of idealism has been common in philosophy
since Plato. Especially well known are Leibniz, Kant, Hegel, and
the English philosophers F. H. Bradley and A. N. Whitehead.

The account of human consciousness and knowledge I give
derives largely from the very traditional school of British empiri-
cists, John Locke, George Berkeley, and David Hume. In that general tradition, some are theists (Berkeley was a bishop) and some
are not (David Hume and another teacher of mine, A. J. Ayer, being probably the best known).

An excellent introduction to scientific accounts of the
brain, written in a very readable style, is *The Brain* (Edinburgh:

Canongate, 2016), by David Eagleman. I do not suggest that he shares all my philosophical views, but I share virtually all his scientific views.

Benjamin Libet's "readiness potential" experiment is described online. His article defending free will is "Do We Have Free Will?" in *The Volitional Brain*, edited by Benjamin Libet, Anthony Freeman, and Keith Sutherland (Exeter: Imprint Academic, 1999). The Pascual-Leone experiment is described in David Eagleman's *The Brain* (p. 103).

The philosopher John Searle, in an article published in 1980, introduced the "Chinese Room" argument. Alone in a room, I could receive sets of Chinese characters through an opening, consult a chart of possible responses, also in Chinese, and send a reply in Chinese. But I might not understand what they mean. This, Searle says, is like what a computer does. The argument has produced a vast set of responses, but it is a picturesque way of putting the point I am making about AI. I should add that Searle is not an idealist, but I think he should be!

Quantum theory, in its most widely accepted interpretation, posits that there are alternative futures that exist, at least at the sub-atomic level. The quantum world is indeterminate. See Carlo Rovelli, *The World Is Not What It Seems* (London: Penguin, 2014), pp. 112 and following. From a philosophical point of view, David Hume remarked that we cannot know or even understand how events could determine only one possible future by some sort of necessity.

PART TWO: COSMOS

The ideas of creativity and emergence have been most clearly stressed in the work of the twentieth-century mathematician and philosopher A. N. Whitehead, the originator of "process philosophy." His work, and that of the British philosopher Stewart Sutherland, convinced me that the notion of divine omnipotence needed to be reformulated, and the idea of human freedom and creativity needed to be more clearly emphasized. An earlier work of mine that tried to do this is: *Rational Theology and the Creativity of God* (Oxford: Blackwell, 1982), especially chapter 6.

I discuss the relation of modern science to philosophy in *The Big Questions in Science and Religion* (West Conshohocken, PA: Templeton Foundation, 2008), and in *Pascal's Fire* (London: Oneworld, 2006). The former is a general survey of the field, while the latter explores more fully the issues discussed briefly in Part Two of the present book. Issues of probability and chance are discussed in my *God, Chance, and Necessity* (London: Oneworld, 1996).

The idea of objective and intrinsic value is discussed in my *Morality, Autonomy, and God* (London: Oneworld, 2013).

Andrew Davis's book, *Mind, Value, and Cosmos* (Washington, DC: Lexington, 2020), provides a valuable analysis of a Whiteheadian view of these matters.

An interesting book by Thomas Nagel, *Mind and Cosmos* (Oxford: Oxford University Press, 2012) follows my general line of argument, though it does not share my more optimistic assessment of cosmic evolution. It is also interesting that his book provoked hate-mail from some materialists! Apparently, intolerance is not only a religious vice.

PART THREE: VIRTUE

The values of truth and understanding, of the creation and appreciation of beauty, and of goodness and love of others, are often known as the three "transcendentals." They are values that express the capacities for thought, feeling, and willing, which are distinctive features of human lives, and they are agreed in many different forms of belief throughout the world.

The idea of beauty as a self-transcending encounter with a non-physical reality is well expressed in Iris Murdoch's *The Sovereignty of Good* (London: Routledge, 1970).

The Beethoven quote is cited in Pitirim A. Sorokin, *The Ways and Power of Love* (Reprint, West Conshohocken, PA: Templeton Foundation, 2015), p. 107.

The quotations from Weinberg are taken from his books, *The First Three Minutes* (London: Andre Deutsch, 1970), p. 149, and *Dreams of a Final Theory* (New York: Vintage, 1993), p. 191.

The philosopher Immanuel Kant, though being skeptical of most traditional "proofs of God," was an idealist, and thought that moral experience was of some reality beyond this sensory world, and that hope for some sort of vindication of virtue, probably beyond this life, was implicit in serious moral commitment. I explored his arguments in *The Development of Kant's View of Ethics* (Oxford: Blackwell, 1972).

PART FOUR: AFTERLIFE

My thinking about hopes of an afterlife can be found in: *Sharing in the Divine Nature* (Eugene, OR: Cascade, 2020), which also criticizes some traditional notions of God.

I have written about the problems facing world religions today in *Religion in the Modern World* (Cambridge: Cambridge University Press, 2019). To what extent contemporary religions can fully support my view is very unclear, though I do happen to be a priest of the Church of England.